SAY IT IN
GERMAN

SAY IT IN
GERMAN

Revised and Enlarged Edition

by Juliette Victor-Rood, Ph.D.

DOVER PUBLICATIONS, INC.
New York

Published in Canada by General Publishing Company, Ltd., 30 Lesmill Road, Don Mills, Toronto, Ontario.
Published in the United Kingdom by Constable and Company, Ltd.

This Dover edition, first published in 1988, is a completely revised and enlarged work, which supersedes the book of the same title originally published by Dover Publications, Inc., in 1950.

This volume was prepared under the editorial supervision of Margalit Fox.

International Standard Book Number: 0-486-20804-4

Manufactured in the United States of America
Dover Publications, Inc., 31 East 2nd Street, Mineola, N.Y. 11501

TABLE OF CONTENTS

INTRODUCTION

German is spoken by about 120 million people in central Europe. It is the official language of the Federal Republic of Germany, the German Democratic Republic, Austria and Liechtenstein. It is one of the four official languages of Switzerland and one of the three official languages of Luxemburg.

While there are many regional dialects, the written language is standard and "colloquial German" is widely understood in cities throughout central Europe. The pronunciation, sentence patterns and idioms given in this book are standard and will be understood by German speakers everywhere. We have also included some regional vocabulary items that will help you if you travel around Germany or go to Austria or Switzerland. Items used in the German Democratic Republic (East Germany) are marked G.D.R.

German is also extensively used as a second language in Europe and *Say It in German* may help you in some places where English is not widely understood, even though German is not an official language there.

NOTES ON THE USE OF THIS BOOK

The words, phrases and sentences in this book have been selected to provide for the communication needs of the traveler or foreign resident in any German-speaking area, and they have been divided into sections corresponding to the situations likely to be encountered in travel and daily life. Those sections which consist of vocabulary lists, such as "Auto: Parts of the Car" and "Gift and Souvenir List," have been alphabetized according to their English entries. However, the sections on food and public notices have been alphabetized according to the German entries to facilitate reference to menus and signs. The index at the back of the book serves as a handy English-German glossary, and helps you to locate quickly a specific word or phrase. With the aid of the index or a bilingual dictionary, many of the sentence patterns included here can be adapted to answer innumerable needs. For example, the place occupied by "six" in the sentence

> I'll wait for your call until [six] o'clock

may be filled with another number in accordance with your needs. In other sentences, the words in square brackets can be replaced with the substitutions immediately following. (These substitutions appear either as bracketed words in the first sentence, or as the indented entries below the first sentence.) Thus, the entry

> These things [to the left] [to the right] belong to me

provides the two sentences: "These things to the left belong to me" and "These things to the right belong to me." Three sentences are provided by the following entries:

> What do you charge [per hour]?
> —per kilometer.
> —per day.

The substitutions taken from within a single entry or from the indented entries following a sentence will always be in the correct grammatical form. Since German nouns, articles, adjectives and verbs take a variety of endings depending on their context, the substitutions you supply yourself from the index or a bilingual dictionary may not always be in the correct form. However, German speakers should have no trouble understanding what you mean. When a word or a phrase in an entry has a different form for a female the feminine form is given in parentheses and marked (F.). Some words (the pronoun "you," for example) have different forms for use in intimate or informal contexts. Occasionally the "familiar" forms are given in parentheses and marked (FAM.). The abbreviation (LIT.) is used when a literal translation of a German phrase or sentence is given in parentheses.

Please note that while brackets always indicate the possibility of substitution, parentheses have been used to provide additional information. They are also used to indicate synonyms or alternative usage for an entry:

Have a seat (OR: Won't you sit down?).

Parentheses may also be used to explain the nuances of a word or phrase or a special usage.

You will notice that the word for "please" has been omitted from many of the sentences of this book. This was done for reasons of space and clarity. To be polite, you should add the word "bitte" (*BIH-tuh*) whenever you would normally say "please" in English.

PRONUNCIATION

Say It in German follows standard High German pronunciation, which is the accepted pronunciation among educated speakers of German throughout the Federal Republic of Germany, the German Democratic Republic, Austria, Switzerland, Liechtenstein and Luxemburg. There are, of course, several different dialects in use throughout these countries, but you will be understood if you follow the pronunciation indicated in this book.

In general, you should pronounce the sounds in the transcription as if they were English. The few sounds in German that have no English equivalents are indicated in the following remarks:

CONSONANTS

German Spelling	Transcription	Remarks
b	b OR p	Like the *b* in Be*r*lin. But at the end of a word or syllable *b* is pronounced *p*.
c	k, ts OR s	Occurs alone only in foreign words. Generally speaking, pronounce as *k* before *a*, *o* or *u*, and pronounce as *ts* or *s* before *e*, *i* and umlauted vowels.

German Spelling	Transcription	Remarks
ch (guttural)	kh	No English equivalent. When it occurs after *a*, *o* or *u*, pronounce it like the *ch* in Ba*ch* or Scottish lo*ch*.
ch (palatal)	$\overline{kh}$	No English equivalent. At the beginning of a word; or after *e*, *i*, *ä*, *ö*, *ü*, *äu* or *eu*; or immediately after consonants, pronounce it like a breathy exaggeration of the *h* in *h*uge.
chs	ks	Usually like the *ks* in loo*ks*, but sometimes $\overline{khs}$ (see *ch*, palatal).
ck	k	Like the *ck* in ba*ck*.
d	d OR t	Like the *d* in *d*og. But at the end of a word or syllable *d* is pronounced *t*.
f	f	Like the *f* in *f*un
g	g, k, $\overline{kh}$ OR zh	Like the *g* in *g*ood. But at the end of a word or syllable *g* is pronounced *k*; after *i*, final *g* is usually pronounced $\overline{kh}$ (see *ch*, palatal). In some foreign words *g* is pronounced like the *g* in French "rouge" (represented as *zh* in our transcription). *G* is always pronounced before *n*.
h	h	Like the *h* in *h*appy. But *h* is silent after a vowel.

German Spelling	Transcription	Remarks
j	y or zh	Like the *y* in *y*et. Never like the *j* in *j*am. Occasionally like the *j* in French "*je*" (represented as *zh* in our transcription).
k	k	Like the *k* in *k*in. *K* is always pronounced before *n*.
l	l	Like the *l* in *l*ift. Never like the "dark" *l* in cool.
m	m	Like the *m* in *m*any.
n	n	Like the *n* in *n*ice.
ng	ng	Like the *ng* in si*ng*er. Never like the *ng* in fi*ng*er.
p	p	Like the *p* in *p*et. *P* is always prounced before *n*.
qu	kv	Like the *kv* in *kv*ass.
r	r	No exact English equivalent. It may be tapped as in Spanish "*pero*," or made in the back of the mouth as in French "*rouge*." The latter sounds like a dry gargle.
s	z, sh or s	Like the *z* in *z*oo at the beginning of a word or before a vowel; like the *sh* of *sh*oe in the combinations *st* and *sp* when they come at the beginning of a word or (usually) a syllable; like the *s* in *s*ign elsewhere.

Remarks

German Spelling   Transcription

German Spelling	Transcription	Remarks
sch	sh	Like the *sh* in *shoe*.
ß	s	Like the *s* in *this*. The ß is a special symbol for *ss*, used in certain circumstances.
t	t	Like the *t* in *time*.
th	t	Like the *t* in *time*.
tsch	ch	Like the *ch* in *church*.
tz	ts	Like the *ts* in *cats*.
v	f or v	Like the *f* in *fun*. In foreign words like *v* in *very*.
w	v	Like the *v* in *very*.
x	ks	Like the *ks* in *looks*.
y	y	As a consonant, like *y* in *York*. Elsewhere, see description under vowels.
z	ts	Like the *ts* in *cats* or *tsetse*.

VOWELS

German Spelling	Transcription	Remarks
a (short)	ah	Like the *a* in *father*, but cut very short.
a (long)	aah	Like the *a* in *father*.
ä (short)	e OR eh	Essentially the same as short stressed German *e*.
ä (long)	ay	Essentially the same as long German *e*.
e (short)	e, eh OR uh	Like the *e* in *pet* when stressed—transcribed *e* in middles of syllables and *eh* at ends of syllables. When unstressed, like the *e* in *busses* (represented as *uh* in our transcription).
e (long)	ay	Like the *a* in *ace*. A pure sound, not a diphthong like the sound in English *ray*, which really consists of two sounds, *ay-ee*.
i (short)	i OR ih	Like the *i* in *hit*. Transcribed *i* in middles of syllables and *ih* at ends of syllables.
i (long)	ee	Like the *ee* in *feet*.
ie	ee	Like the *ee* in *feet*.

Remarks

German Spelling	Transcription	Remarks
o (short)	aw	Like the *aw* in *awful*, but cut very short.
o (long)	oh	Like the *o* in *road*. A pure sound, not a diphthong like the sound in English *so*, which really consists of two sounds, *oh-ōo*.
ö (short)	ur	No English equivalent. Do not pronounce the *r* itself. Round your lips to say *oh*, and without changing the position of the lips, say *eh*.
ö (long)	ūr	No English equivalent. Same as short *ö*, but held longer.
u (short)	oo	Like the *oo* in *foot*.
u (long)	ōo	Like the *oo* in *moon*.
ü (short)	ew	No English equivalent. As in French "*Luc.*" Round your lips to say *ōo*, and without changing the position of the lips, say *ee*.
ü (long)	ēw	No English equivalent. Like short *ü*, but held longer.
y	ew, i or ih	Normally restricted to foreign words. Pronounce as *ü* or as in the original language.

DIPHTHONGS

German Spelling	Transcription	Remarks
ai, ay, ei, ey	ī	Like the *i* in *bite*.
au	ow	Like the *ow* in *how*. Never as in *low*.
äu, eu	oy	Like the *oy* in *toy*.

SAY IT IN
GERMAN

EVERYDAY PHRASES

1. Hi (informal).   Tag.*   *taahk.*

2. Good morning.   Guten Morgen.
GOO-tuhn MAWR-guhn.

3. Good day (OR: **Hello; Good afternoon**).
Guten Tag.†   *GOO-tuhn taahk.*

4. Good evening.   Guten Abend.
GOO-tuhn AAH-buhnt.

5. Good night (said only on going to bed).
Gute Nacht.   *GOO-tuh nahkht.*

6. Welcome!   Willkommen!   *vil-KAW-muhn!*

7. Goodbye (LIT.: **Till [we] see [each other] again**).
Auf Wiedersehen.‡   *owf VEE-duhr-zayn.*

8. 'Bye (informal).   Tschüs.§   *chews.*

9. See you (LIT.: **Until**) **[later] [soon].**
Bis [später] [bald].   *bis [SHPAY-tuhr] [bahlt].*

10. [Very] pleased to meet you.
[Sehr] angenehm (OR: Es freut mich).
[zayr] AHN-guh-naym (OR: es froyt mikh).

11. Yes.   Ja.   *yaah.*

12. No.   Nein.   *nīn.*

---

*In southern Germany and Austria: Servus (*ZAYR-voos*). In Switzerland: Grüezi. (*GREW-eh-tsih*).

†In southern Germany and Austria: Grüß Gott (*grews gawt*). In Switzerland: Grüezi.

‡In southern Germany and Austria: Auf Wiederschauen (*owf VEE-duhr-shown*).

§In southern Germany and Austria: Servus OR Pfüeti (*ZAYR-voos* OR *PFEW-uh-tee*). In Switzerland: Tschau (*chow*).

13. Perhaps (OR: Maybe).   Vielleicht.   *fee-LĪKHT.*

14. Please.   Bitte.   *BIH-tuh.*

15. Allow me (OR: May I?).
Gestatten Sie? (OR: Darf ich?)
guh-SHTAH-tuhn zee? (OR: dahrf ikh?)

16. Excuse me.   Entschuldigen Sie!
ent-SHOOL-dih-guhn zee!

17. Thanks [very much].   Danke [sehr].***
DAHNG-kuh [zayr].

18. You're welcome (OR: Don't mention it).
Bitte.   *BIH-tuh.*

19. All right (OR: Fine, very good).
In Ordnung (OR: Gut).   *in AWRD-noong (OR: gōot).*

20. It doesn't matter.   Das macht nichts.
dahs mahkht nĭkhts.

21. Don't bother.   Bemühen Sie sich nicht!
buh-MEW-uhn zee zikh nĭkht!

22. I'm sorry.   Es tut mir leid.   *es tōot meer līt.*

23. You've been very kind.
Sie sind sehr freundlich gewesen.
zee zint zayr FROYNT-likh guh-VAY-zuhn.

24. You've been very helpful (LIT.: That was a big help).
Das war eine große Hilfe.
dahs vaahr Ī-nuh GROH-suh HIL-fuh.

25. Come in.   Kommen Sie herein!
KAW-muhn zee heh-RĪN!

26. Come here.   Kommen Sie her!
KAW-muhn zee hayr!

*In Switzerland: Merci [vielmals] (*MER-see [FEEL-maahls]*).

27. Come with me.   Kommen Sie mit mir!
KAW-muhn zee mit meer!

28. Come back later.   Kommen Sie später zurück!
KAW-muhn zee SHPAY-tuhr tsoo-REWK!

29. Come early.   Kommen Sie früh!
KAW-muhn zee frew!

30. Wait a moment.
Warten Sie einen Moment (OR: Augenblick)!
VAHR-tuhn zee Ī-nuhn moh-MENT (OR: OW-guhn-blik)!

31. Wait for us.   Warten Sie auf uns!
VAHR-tuhn zee owf oons!

32. Not yet.   Noch nicht.   *nawkh nikht.*

33. Not now.   Jetzt nicht.   *yetst nikht.*

34. Listen!   Hören Sie zu!
HUR-ruhn zee tsoo!

35. Look out!   Passen Sie auf!   *PAH-suhn zee owf!*

36. Be careful!   Seien Sie vorsichtig! (OR: Vorsicht!)
ZĪ-uhn zee FOHR-zikh-tikh! (OR: FOHR-zikht!)

SOCIAL PHRASES

37. May I introduce [Mr. Müller]?
Darf ich bekanntmachen (OR: vorstellen); das ist [Herr Müller].
dahrf ikh buh-KAHNT-mah-khuhn (OR: FOHR-shteh-luhn); dahs ist her MEW-luhr.

38. —Mrs. Huber.   —Frau Huber.
—frow HOO-buhr.

39. —**Miss Schulz.**   —Fräulein* Schulz.
—*FROY-lĭn shoolts.*

40. How are you?†
Wie geht es Ihnen? (OR: Wie geht's?)
vee gayt es EE-nuhn? (OR: vee gayts?)

41. Very well, thanks, and you?
Danke gut und Ihnen?
DAHNG-kuh gōōt oont EE-nuhn?

42. How are things?   Was gibt's sonst?
vahs geepts zawnst?

43. So, so.   Es geht.   *es gayt.*

44. What's new?   Was gibt's Neues?
vahs geepts NOY-uhs?

45. Have a seat (OR: Won't you sit down?).
Nehmen Sie Platz!   *NAY-muhn zee plahts!*

46. It's a pleasure to see you again.
Es freut mich, Sie wiederzusehen.
es froyt mĭkh, zee VEE-duhr-tsōō-zay-uhn.

47. Congratulations.   Gratuliere.
grah-too-LEE-ruh.

48. All the best.   Alles Gute!   *AH-luhs GŌŌ-tuh!*

49. I like you very much.
Ich habe Sie (FAM.: dich) sehr gern.
ĭkh HAAH-buh zee (FAM.: dĭkh) zayr gern.

50. I love you.   Ich liebe dich.   *ĭkh LEE-buh dĭkh.*

---

*Most women now prefer to be addressed with the title "Frau," regardless of their marital status.

†Only ask this of people you already know, not of people you have just met.

51. May I see you again? Darf ich Sie wiedersehen?
dahrf ikh zee VEE-duhr-zay-uhn?

52. Let's make a date for next week.
Machen wir eine Verabredung für nächste Woche!
MAH-khuhn veer Ī-nuh fer-AHP-ray-doong fewr NAYKH-stuh VAW-khuh!

53. I've enjoyed myself very much (OR: **I had a good time**).
Ich habe mich gut amüsiert.
ikh HAAH-buh mikh goot ah-mew-ZEERT.

54. Give my regards to [your boyfriend] [your girlfriend].
Grüßen Sie [Ihren Freund] [Ihre Freundin] von mir!
GREW-suhn zee [EE-ruhn froynt] [EE-ruh FROYN-din] fawn meer!

See also "Family," p. 159.

BASIC QUESTIONS

55. What? Was? *vahs?*

56. What did you say? (OR: **Pardon (me)?**)
Wie bitte? *vee BIH-tuh?*

57. What's [that] [this]? Was ist [das] [dies]?
vahs ist [dahs] [dees]?

58. What must I do? Was muß ich tun?
vahs moos ikh toon?

59. What's the matter? (OR: **What's wrong?**)
Was ist los? *vahs ist lohs?*

60. What do you want (OR: wish)?
Was wollen (OR: wünschen) Sie?
vahs VAW-luhn (OR: WEWN-shuhn) zee?

61. When?   Wann?   *vahn?*

62. When [does it leave]?   Wann [fährt es ab]?
vahn [fayrt es ahp]?

63. —does it arrive.   —kommt es an.
—kawmt es ahn.

64. —does it begin.   —fängt es an.
—fengkt es ahn.

65. —does it end.   —geht es zu Ende.
—gayt es tsoo EN-duh.

66. Where?   Wo?   *voh?*

67. Where is it?   Wo ist es?   *voh ist es?*

68. Why?   Warum?   *vah-ROOM?*

69. How?   Wie?   *vee?*

70. How long?   Wie lange?   *vee LAHNG-uh?*

71. How far?   Wie weit?   *vee vīt?*

72. How much?   Wieviel?
vee-FEEL? (OR: VEE-feel?)

73. How many?   Wieviele?   *vee-FEE-luh?*

74. How do you do that?   Wie macht man das?
vee mahkht mahn dahs?

75. How does it work?   Wie funktioniert es?
vee foongk-tsee-oh-NEERT es?

76. Who?   Wer?   *vayr?*

77. Who are you?   Wer sind Sie?   *vayr zint zee?*

78. Who is [that boy]?   Wer ist [der Junge* da]?
vayr ist [dayr YOONG-uh daah]?

79. —that girl.   —das Mädchen† da.
—dahs MAYT-khuhn daah.

80. —this man.   —dieser Mann.
—DEE-zuhr mahn.

81. —this woman.   —diese Frau.   *—DEE-zuh frow.*

82. Am I [on time]?   Bin ich [pünktlich]?
bin ikh [PEWNGKT-likh]?

83. —early.   —früh.   *frew.*

84. —late.   —spät.   *—shpayt.*

TALKING ABOUT YOURSELF

85. What's your name?
Wie heißen Sie? (OR: Was ist Ihr Name?)
vee HĪ-suhn zee? (OR: vahs ist eer NAAH-muh?)

86. I'm Mr. Schulz.   Ich bin Herr Schulz.
ikh bin her shoolts.

87. My name is [John].   Ich heiße [John].
ikh HĪ-suh ["John"].

88. I'm [21] years old.
Ich bin [einundzwanzig] Jahre alt.
ikh bin [ĪN-oont-tsvahn-tsikh] YAAH-ruh ahlt.

89. I'm [an American citizen].
Ich bin [Bürger der Vereinigten Staaten].
ikh bin [BEWR-guhr dayr fayr-Ī-nikh-tuhn SHTAAH-tuhn].

*In southern Germany, Austria and Switzerland: der Bub
(*dayr bōop*).

†In southern Germany and Austria: Mädel (*MAY-duhl*). In
Switzerland: Maitli (*MĪT-lee*).

90. My address is [35 Main St.].
Meine Adresse ist [Hauptstraße fünfunddreißig].
MĪ-nuh ah-DREH-suh ist [HOWPT-shtraah-suh FEWNF-oont-drī-sikh].

91. I'm [a student].
Ich bin [Student (F.: Studentin)].
ikh bin [shtoo-DENT (F.: shtoo-DEN-tin)].

92. —a teacher. —Lehrer (F.: Lehrerin).
—LAY-ruhr (F.: LAY-ruh-rin).

93. —a businessperson.
—Geschäftsmann (F.: Geschäftsfrau).
—guh-SHEFTS-mahn (F.: guh-SHEFTS-frow).

94. What's your job? (OR: What do you do?)
Was ist Ihr Beruf? *vahs ist eer buh-ROOF?*

95. I'm a friend of [Ernst].
Ich bin ein Freund (F.: eine Freundin) von [Ernst].
ikh bin īn froynt (F.: Ī-nuh FROYN-din) fawn [ernst].

96. [He] [She] works for [Siemens].
[Er] [Sie] arbeitet bei [Siemens].
[ayr] [zee] AHR-bī-tuht bī [ZEE-muhns].

97. I'm here [on vacation].
Ich bin hier [auf Ferien].*
ikh bin heer [owf FAY-ree-uhn].

98. —on a business trip. —auf einer Geschäftsreise.
—owf Ī-nuhr guh-SHEFTS-rī-zuh.

99. I've been here [one week].
Ich bin seit [einer Woche] hier.
ikh bin zīt [Ī-nuhr VAW-khuh] heer.

*In general: "Ferien" for professors, teachers, students; "Urlaub" (*OOR-lowp*) for workers.

100. We plan to stay here until [Friday].
Wir haben vor, bis [Freitag] hier zu bleiben.
veer HAAH-buhn fohr, bis [FRĪ-taahk] heer tsōō BLĪ-buhn.

101. I'm traveling to [Vienna].
Ich reise nach [Wien].
ikh RĪ-zuh naahkh [veen].

102. I'm in a hurry. __ Ich habe es eilig.
ikh HAAH-buh es Ī-likh.

103. I'm [cold] [warm]. Es ist mir [kalt] [warm].
es ist meer [kahlt] [vahrm].

104. I'm [hungry] [thirsty].
Ich habe [Hunger] [Durst].
ikh HAAH-buh [HOONG-uhr] [doorst].

105. I'm [busy]. Ich bin [beschäftigt].
ikh bin [buh-SHEF-tikht].

106. —tired. —müde. *—MEW-duh.*

107. —glad. —froh. *—froh.*

108. —disappointed. —enttäuscht.
—ent-TOYSHT.

109. I can't do it. Ich kann das nicht machen.
ikh kahn dahs nikht MAH-khuhn.

110. We're [happy]. __ Wir sind [glücklich].
veer zint [GLEWK-likh].

111. —unhappy. —unglücklich.
—OON-glewk-likh.

112. —angry. —böse. *—BŪR-zuh.*

MAKING YOURSELF UNDERSTOOD

113. Do you speak [English]?
Sprechen Sie [Englisch]?
SHPREH-khuhn zee [ENG-lish]?

114. Where is [English] spoken?
Wo spricht man [Englisch]?
voh shprikht mahn [ENG-lish]?

115. Does anyone here speak [French]?
Spricht hier jemand [Französisch]?
shprikht heer YAY-mahnt [frahn-TSUR-zish]?

116. I read only [Italian].
Ich lese nur [Italienisch].
ikh LAY-zuh noor [ee-tahl-YAY-nish].

117. I speak a little [German].
Ich kann ein bißchen* (OR: ein wenig) [Deutsch].
ikh kahn īn BIS-khuhn (OR: īn VAY-nikh) [doych].

118. Speak more slowly.   Sprechen Sie langsamer!
SHPREH-khuhn zee LAHNG-zaah-muhr!

119. I [don't] understand.   Ich verstehe [nicht].
ikh fer-SHTAY-uh [nikht].

120. Do you understand me?   Verstehen Sie mich?
fer-SHTAY-uhn zee mikh?

121. I [don't] know.   Ich weiß [nicht].
ikh vīs [nikht].

122. I think so.   Ich glaube ja.
ikh GLOW-buh yaah.

123. Repeat it.   Wiederholen Sie es!
vee-duhr-HOH-luhn zee es!

---

*In Austria: ein bisse(r)l (*īn BIH-suh(r)l*).

124. Write it down. Schreiben Sie es auf!
SHRĪ-buhn zee es owf!

125. Answer "yes" or "no."
Sagen Sie "ja" oder "nein!"
ZAAH-guhn zee "yaah" OH-duhr "nīn!"

126. You're [right] [wrong].
Sie haben [recht] [unrecht].
zee HAAH-buhn [rekht] [OON-rekht].

127. What does [this word] mean?
Was bedeutet [dieses Wort]?
vahs buh-DOY-tuht [DEE-zuhs vort]?

128. How do you say ["pencil"] in German?
Wie sagt man ["pencil"] auf deutsch?
vee zaahkt mahn ["pencil"] owf doych?

129. How do you spell [Osnabrück]?
Wie buchstabiert man [Osnabrück]?
vee bookh-shtah-BEERT mahn [AWS-nah-brewk]?

DIFFICULTIES AND MISUNDERSTANDINGS

130. Where is [the American Embassy]?
Wo ist [die amerikanische Botschaft]?
voh ist [dee ah-may-ree-KAAH-nih-shuh BOHT-shahft]?

131. —the police station. —die Polizeiwache.
—dee poh-lee-TSĪ-vah-khuh.

132. —the lost-and-found office. —das Fundbüro.
—dahs FOONT-bew-roh.

12 DIFFICULTIES, MISUNDERSTANDINGS

133. I want to talk to [the manager] [your superior].
Ich möchte mit [dem Geschäftsführer] [Ihrem
_Vorgesetzten] sprechen.
*ikh MURKH-tuh mit [daym guh-SHEFTS-few-ruhr]
[EE-ruhm FOHR-guh-zets-tuhn] SHPREH-khuhn.*

134. Can you help me?   Können Sie mir helfen?
KUR-nuhn zee meer HEL-fuhn?

135. Can you tell me how to get there?
Können Sie mir sagen, wie ich hinkomme?
*KUR-nuhn zee meer ZAAH-guhn, vee ikh HIN-kaw-
muh?*

136. I'm looking for my (LIT.: a) friend.
Ich suche einen Freund (F.: eine Freundin).
ikh ZOO-khuh Ī-nuhn froynt (F.: Ī-nuh FROYN-din).

137. I'm lost.   Ich habe mich verirrt.
ikh HAAH-buh mikh fer-IRT.

138. I can't find [the address].
Ich kann [die Adresse] nicht finden.
ikh kahn [dee ah-DREH-suh] nikht FIN-duhn.

139. She has lost [her handbag].
Sie hat [ihre Handtasche] verloren.
zee haaht [EE-ruh HAHNT-tah-shuh] fer-LOH-ruhn.

140. We forgot [our keys].
Wir haben [unsere Schlüssel] vergessen.
*veer HAAH-buhn [OON-zuh-ruh SHLEW-suhl] fer-
GEH-suhn.*

141. We missed [the train].
Wir haben [den Zug] verpaßt.
veer HAAH-buhn [dayn tsook] fer-PAHST.

142. It's not my fault.   Es ist nicht meine Schuld.
es ist nikht MĪ-nuh shoolt.

143. I don't remember [the name].
Ich kann mich an [den Namen] nicht erinnern.
ikh kahn mikh ahn [dayn NAAH-muhn] nikht ayr-IH-nuhrn.

144. What shall I do?   Was soll ich machen?
vahs zawl ikh MAH-khuhn?

145. Leave us alone!   Lassen Sie uns in Ruhe!
LAH-suhn zee oons in ROO-uh!

146. Go away!   Gehen Sie weg!
GAY-uhn zee vek!

147. Help!   Hilfe!   *HIL-fuh!*

148. Police!   Polizei!   *poh-lee-TSĪ!*

149. Thief!   Dieb!   *deep!*

150. Fire!   Feuer!   *FOY-uhr!*

151. This is an emergency.   Es ist ein Notfall.
es ist īn NOHT-fahl.

CUSTOMS

152. Where is [the customs office]?
Wo ist [das Zollamt]?
voh ist [dahs TSAWL-ahmt]?

153. Here is [our baggage].
Hier ist [unser Gepäck].
heer ist [OON-zuhr guh-PEK].

154. —my passport.   —mein Paß.   *—mīn pahs.*

155. —my identification card.
—mein Ausweis (OR: Personalausweis).
—mīn OWS-vīs (OR: per-zoh-NAAHL-ows-vīs).

156. —my health certificate.
—mein ärztliches Attest.
—mīn AYRTST-lih-khuhs ah-TEST.

157. —my visitor's visa.
—mein Visum (OR: Touristenvisum).
—mīn VEE-zoom (OR: tōō-RIS-tuhn-vee-zoom).

158. I'm in transit.
Ich bin auf der Durchreise.
ikh bin owf dayr DOORKH-rī-zuh.

159. [The bags] over there are mine.
[Die Koffer] da drüben sind die meinen.
[dee KAW-fuhr] dah DREW-buhn zint dee MĪ-nuhn.

160. Must I open everything?
Muß ich alles öffnen?
moos ikh AH-luhs URF-nuhn?

161. I can't open the trunk.
Ich kann den Koffer nicht öffnen.
ikh kahn dayn KAW-fuhr nikht URF-nuhn.

162. There's nothing here but [clothing].
Es sind hier nur [Kleidungsstücke].
es zint heer nōōr [KLĪ-doongs-shtew-kuh].

163. I have nothing to declare.
Ich habe nichts zu verzollen.
ikh HAAH-buh nikhts tsōō fer-TSAW-luhn.

164. Everything is for my personal use.
Alles ist für meinen persönlichen Gebrauch.
AH-luhs ist fewr MĪ-nuhn per-ZURN-lih-khuhn guh-
   BROWKH.

165. I bought [this necklace] in the United States.
Ich habe [dieses Halsband] in den Vereinigten Staaten
gekauft.
*ikh HAAH-buh [DEE-zuhs HAHLS-bahnt] in dayn
fer-Ī-nikh-tuhn SHTAAH-tuhn guh-KOWFT.*

166. These are [gifts].   Diese sind [Geschenke].
DEE-zuh zint [guh-SHENG-kuh].

167. This is all I have.
Dies ist alles, was ich habe.
dees ist AH-luhs, vahs ikh HAAH-buh.

168. Must duty be paid on [these goods]? (LIT.: Are
[these goods] dutiable?)
Sind [diese Waren] zollpflichtig?
zint [DEE-zuh VAAH-ruhn] TSAWL-pflikh-tikh?

169. Are you finished?   Sind Sie fertig?
zint zee FER-tikh?

BAGGAGE

**170. Where can we check our luggage through to
[Geneva]?**
Wo können wir unser Gepäck bis nach [Genf]
aufgeben?
*voh KUR-nuhn veer OON-zuhr guh-PEK bis naahkh
[genf] OWF-gay-buhn?*

**171. These things [to the left] [to the right] belong to
me.**
Diese Sachen [links] [rechts] gehören mir.
*DEE-zuh ZAH-khuhn [lingks] [rekhts] guh-HUR-ruhn
meer.*

172. I can't find all my baggage.
Ich kann nicht alle meine Gepäckstücke finden.
*ikh kahn nikht AH-luh MĪ-nuh guh-PEK-shtew-kuh
FIN-duhn.*

173. One [of my packages] is missing.
Eins [meiner Pakete] fehlt.
īns [MĪ-nuhr pah-KAY-tuh] faylt.

174. I want to leave [this suitcase] here [for a few days].
Ich möchte [diesen Koffer] [einige Tage] hier lassen.
*ikh MURKH-tuh [DEE-zuhn KAW-fuhr] [Ī-nih-guh
TAAH-guh] heer LAH-suhn.*

175. Give me a claim check for the baggage.
Geben Sie mir einen Gepäckschein!
GAY-buhn zee meer Ī-nuhn guh-PEK-shīn!

176. I have [a black trunk] [four pieces of luggage altogether].
Ich habe [einen schwarzen Koffer] [insgesamt vier Stück Gepäck].
*ikh HAAH-buh [Ī-nuhn SHVAHR-tsuhn KAW-fuhr]
[ins-guh-ZAMT feer shtewk guh-PEK].*

177. Carry this to the baggage room.
Bringen Sie dies zur Gepäckaufbewahrung!
*BRING-uhn zee dees tso͞or guh-PEK-owf-buh-vaah-
roong!*

178. Don't forget that.   Vergessen Sie das nicht!
fer-GEH-suhn zee dahs nikht!

179. I'll carry this myself.   Ich trage dies selbst.
ikh TRAAH-guh dees zelpst.

180. Follow me.   Folgen Sie mir!
FAWL-guhn zee meer!

181. Get me [a taxi] [a porter].
Besorgen Sie mir [ein Taxi] [einen Gepäckträger]!
buh-ZAWR-guhn zee meer [īn TAH-ksee] [Ī-nuhn guh-PEK-tray-guhr]!

182. This is very fragile.
Dies ist sehr zerbrechlich.
dees ist zayr tser-BREKH-likh.

183. Handle this carefully.
Behandeln Sie dies sehr vorsichtig!
buh-HAHN-duhln zee dees zayr FOHR-zikh-tikh!

184. How much do I owe (you)?
Wieviel bin ich schuldig?
VEE-feel bin ikh SHOOL-dikh?

185. What is the customary tip?
Was ist das übliche Trinkgeld?
vahs ist dahs EWP-lih-khuh TRINGK-gelt?

TRAVEL DIRECTIONS

186. I want to go [to the airline office].
Ich möchte [zum Büro der Fluglinie] gehen.*
ikh MURKH-tuh [tsoom bew-ROH dayr FLOOK-lee-nee-uh] GAY-uhn.

187. —to the travel agency. —zum Reisebüro.
—tsoom RĪ-zuh-bew-roh.

*"Gehen" is used only for walking. Use "fahren" *(FAAH-ruhn)* for driving or riding in a vehicle.

188. —to the [Austrian/German/Swiss] (national tourist) information office.

—zum [österreichischen/deutschen/schweizerischen (OR: schweizer)] Auskunftsbüro.

—tsoom [ŪRS-tuh-rī-khih-shuhn/DOY-chuhn/SHVĪ-tsuh-rih-shuhn (OR: SHVĪ-tsuhr)] OWS-koonfts-bēw-roh.

189. How long does it take to walk [to the Prater]?

Wie lange dauert es zu Fuß [zum Prater]?

vee LAHNG-uh DOW-uhrt es tsōō foos [tsoom PRAAH-tuhr]?

190. Is this the shortest way [to the castle]?

Ist dies der kürzeste Weg [zum Schloß]?

ist dees dayr KEWR-tsuhs-tuh vayk [tsoom shlaws]?

191. Show me the way [to the center of town] [to the shopping district].

Zeigen Sie mir den Weg [zum Stadtzentrum] [zum Einkaufszentrum]!

TSĪ-guhn zee meer dayn vayk [tsoom SHTAHT-tsen-troom] [tsoom ĪN-kowfs-tsen-troom]!

192. Should I turn to the [north]?

Soll ich nach [Norden] abbiegen?

zawl ikh naahkh [NAWR-duhn] AHP-bee-guhn?

193. —south.   —Süden.   —ZEW-duhn.

194. —east.   —Osten.   —AWS-tuhn.

195. —west.   —Westen.   —VES-tuhn.

196. [What street] is this?

[Welche Straße] ist dies?

[VEL-khuh SHTRAAH-suh] ist dees?

197. How far is it from here?

Wie weit ist es von hier aus?

vee vīt ist es fawn heer ows?

198. Is it near or far?   Ist es nahe oder weit?
ist es NAAH-uh OH-duhr vīt?

199. Can we walk there?
Können wir dahin zu Fuß (gehen)?
KUR-nuhn veer daah-HIN tsoo foos (GAY-uhn)?

200. Am I going in the right direction?
Gehe ich in die richtige Richtung?
GAY-uh ikh in dee RIKH-tih-guh RIKH-toong?

201. Please point.
Bitte deuten Sie mit dem Finger darauf hin!
BIH-tuh DOY-tuhn zee mit daym FING-uhr DAAH-rowf hin!

202. Should I go [this way] [that way]?
Soll ich [hier entlang] [dort entlang] (gehen)?
zawl ikh [heer ent-LAHNG] [dawrt ent-LAHNG] (GAY-uhn)?

203. Turn [left] [right] at the next corner.
An der nächsten Ecke biegen Sie [nach links] [nach rechts] ab!
ahn dayr NAYKH-stuhn EH-kuh BEE-guhn zee [naahkh lingks] [naahkh rekhts] ahp!

204. Is it [on this side of the street]?
Ist es [auf dieser Seite der Straße]?
ist es [owf DEE-zuhr ZĪ-tuh dayr SHTRAAH-suh]?

205. —on the other side of the street.
—auf der anderen Seite der Straße.
—owf dayr AHN-duh-ruhn ZĪ-tuh dayr SHTRAAH-suh.

206. —across the bridge.
—auf der anderen Seite der Brücke.
—owf dayr AHN-duh-ruhn ZĪ-tuh dayr BREW-kuh.

207. —along the boulevard.
—den Boulevard entlang.
—*dayn bōo-luh-VAAHR ent-LAHNG.*

208. —between these avenues.
—zwischen diesen Alleen.
—*TSVIH-shuhn DEE-zuhn ah-LAY-uhn.*

209. —beyond the traffic light.
—weiter als die Verkehrsampel.
—*VĪ-tuhr ahls dee fer-KAYRS-ahm-puhl.*

210. —next to the apartment house.
—neben dem Wohnhaus.
—*NAY-buhn daym VOHN-hows.*

211. —in the middle of the block.
—in der Mitte des Blocks.
—*in dayr MIH-tuh des blawks.*

212. —straight ahead.   —geradeaus.
—*guh-RAAH-duh-ows.*

213. —inside the train station.   —im Bahnhof.
—*im BAAHN-hohf.*

214. —near the square.   —bei dem Platz.
bī daym plahts.

215. outside the lobby.   —außerhalb der Vorhalle.
—*OW-suhr-hahlp dayr FOHR-hah-luh.*

216. —at the entrance.   —beim Eingang.
—*bīm ĪN-gahng.*

217. —opposite the park.   —gegenüber vom Park.
—*gay-guhn-EW-buhr fawm pahrk.*

218. —next to the school.
—neben der Schule.
—*NAY-buhn dayr SHOO-luh.*

219. —in front of the monument.
—vor dem Denkmal.
—*fohr daym DENGK-maahl.*

220. —in (OR: at) the rear of the store.
—hinten im Laden.   —*HIN-tuhn im LAAH-duhn.*

221. —behind the building.   —hinter dem Gebäude.
—*HIN-tuhr daym guh-BOY-duh.*

222. —up the hill.   —den Berg hinauf.
—*dayn berk hih-NOWF.*

223. —down the stairs.   —die Treppe hinunter.
—*dee TREH-puh hih-NOON-tuhr.*

224. —at the top of the escalator.
—oben auf der Rolltreppe.
—*OH-buhn owf dayr RAWL-treh-puh.*

225. —around the traffic circle.
—um den Kreisverkehr.
—*oom dayn KRĪS-fer-kayr.*

226. Factory. Fabrik.   *fah-BREEK.*

227. Office building.
Geschäftshaus (OR: Geschäftsgebäude).
guh-SHEFTS-hows (OR: guh-SHEFTS-guh-boy-duh).

228. Residential section.   Wohnviertel.
VOHN-feer-tuhl.

229. Suburb. Vorort.   *FOHR-awrt.*

230. City. Stadt.   *shtaht.*

231. In the country (side).
Auf dem Lande.   *owf daym LAHN-duh.*

232. Village. Dorf.   *dawrf.*

BOAT

233. When must I go on board?
Wann muß ich an Bord gehen?
vahn moos ikh ahn bawrt GAY-uhn?

234. Bon voyage! Gute Reise! *GOO-tuh RĪ-zuh!*

235. I'd like to rent a deck chair.
Ich möchte einen Liegestuhl mieten.
ikh MURKH-tuh Ī-nuhn LEE-guh-shtool MEE-tuhn.

236. Can we go ashore [at Cologne]?
Können wir [in Köln] an Land gehen?
KUR-nuhn veer [in kurln] ahn lahnt GAY-uhn?

237. At what time is breakfast served?
Um wieviel Uhr wird das Frühstück serviert?
oom VEE-feel oor virt dahs FREW-shtewk zer-VEERT?

238. When is the [noon meal] [evening meal]?
Wann ist das [Mittagessen] [Abendessen]?
vahn ist dahs [MIH-taahk-eh-suhn] [AAH-buhnt-eh-suhn]?

239. I feel seasick. Ich bin seekrank.
ikh bin ZAY-krahngk.

240. Do you have a remedy for seasickness?
Haben Sie eine Arznei gegen Seekrankheit?
HAAH-buhn zee Ī-nuh ahrts-NĪ GAY-guhn ZAY-krahngk-hīt?

241. Lifeboat. Rettungsboot. *REH-toongs-boht.*

242. Life preserver (OR: Life jacket).
Schwimmweste. *SHVIM-veh-stuh.*

243. Ferry. Fähre. *FAY-ruh.*

244. Dock. Dock. *dawk.*

245. Cabin. Kabine. *kah-BEE-nuh.*

246. Deck. Deck. *dek.*

247. Gymnasium. Turnhalle. *TOORN-hah-luh.*

248. Swimming pool. Schwimmbad.
SHVIM-baaht.

249. Captain. Kapitän. *kah-pee-TAYN.*

250. Purser. Zahlmeister. *TSAAHL-mīs-tuhr.*

251. Cabin steward. Kabinensteward.
kah-BEE-nuhn-"steward."

252. Dining-room steward. Speisesaalsteward.
SHPĪ-zuh-zaahl-"steward."

AIRPLANE

253. I want to make a reservation.
Ich möchte einen Flug buchen. ___
ikh MURKH-tuh Ī-nuhn flook BOO-khuhn.

254. I want to cancel my reservation.
Ich möchte meine Buchung stornieren.
ikh MURKH-tuh MĪ-nuh BOO-khoong shtawr-NEE-ruhn.

255. When's the next flight to [Zurich]?
Wann ist der nächste Flug nach [Zürich]?
vahn ist dayr NAYKH-stuh flook naahkh [TSEW-rikh]?

256. When does the plane land at [Munich]?
Wann landet die Maschine in [München]?
vahn LAHN-duht dee mah-SHEE-nuh in MEWN-khuhn]?

257. What kind of plane is used on that flight?
Was für eine Maschine gebraucht man auf dem Flug?
*vahs fewr Ī-nuh mah-SHEE-nuh guh-BROWKHT
mahn owf daym flook?*

258. Will food be served? Wird Essen serviert?
Virt EH-suhn zer-VEERT?

259. May I confirm the reservation by telephone?
Darf ich die Buchung telefonisch bestätigen?
*dahrf ikh dee BOO-khoong tay-lay-FOH-nish buh-
SHTAY-tih-guhn?*

260. At what time should we check in [at the airport]?
Um wieviel Uhr sollen wir uns [beim Flughafen]
melden?
*oom VEE-feel ōōr ZAW-luhn veer oons [bīm FLŌŌK-
haah-fuhn] MEL-duhn?*

**261. How long does it take to get to the airport from
my hotel?**
Wie lange dauert es zum Flughafen von meinem
Hotel?
*vee LAHNG-uh DOW-uhrt es tsoom FLŌŌK-haah-
fuhn fawn MĪ-nuhm hoh-TEL?*

**262. Is there bus service between the airport and the
city?**
Gibt es einen Zubringerdienst zwischen dem Flughafen
und der Stadt?
*geept es Ī-nuhn TSŌŌ-bring-uhr-deenst TSVIH-shuhn
daym FLŌŌK-haah-fuhn oont dayr shtaht?*

263. Is that flight [nonstop] [direct]?
Ist der Flug [ohne Zwischenlandungen] [direkt]?
*ist dayr flook [OH-nuh TSVIH-shuhn-lahn-doong-uhn]
[dee-REKT]?*

264. Where does the plane stop en route?
Wo landet die Maschine unterwegs?
voh LAHN-duht dee mah-SHEE-nuh oon-tuhr-VAYKS?

265. How long do we stop here?
Wie lange bleiben wir hier?
vee LANG-uh BLĪ-buhn veer heer?

266. May I stop over in [Stuttgart]?
Darf ich meine Reise in [Stuttgart] unterbrechen?
dahrf ĭkh MĪ-nuh RĪ-zuh in [SHTOOT-gahrt] oon-tuhr-BREH-khuhn?

267. We want to travel [first class] [economy (OR: second) class].
Wir möchten [erster Klasse] [zweiter Klasse] reisen.
veer MURKH-tuhn [AYRS-tuhr KLAH-suh] [TSVĪ-tuhr KLAH-suh] RĪ-zuhn.

268. Is flight number [22] on time?
Landet Flugnummer [zweiundzwanzig] rechtzeitig?
LAHN-duht FLOOK-noo-muhr [TSVĪ-oont-tsvahn-tsĭkh] REKHT-tsī-tikh?

269. How much baggage may I take along?
Wieviel Gepäck darf ich mitnehmen?
VEE-feel guh-PEK dahrf ĭkh MIT-nay-muhn?

270. How much per kilo for excess (weight)?
Wieviel kostet Übergewicht pro Kilo?
VEE-feel KAWS-tuht EW-buhr-guh-vikht proh KEE-loh?

271. May I carry this on board?
Darf ich dies an Bord tragen?
dahrf ĭkh dees ahn bawrt TRAAH-guhn?

272. I'd like a seat [on the aisle].
Ich möchte einen Platz [am Gang].
ikh MURKH-tuh Ī-nuhn plahts [ahm gahng].

273. —by a window.   —an einem Fenster.
—ahn Ī-nuhm FEN-stuhr.

274. —by the emergency exit.
—neben dem Notausgang.
—NAY-buhn daym NOHT-ows-gahng.

275. May we board the plane now?
Dürfen wir jetzt einsteigen?
DEWR-fuhn veer yetst IN-shtī-guhn?

276. From which gate does my flight leave?
Von welchem Flugsteig fliegt mein Flug ab?
fawn VEL-khuhm FLOOK-shtīk fleekt mīn flook ahp?

277. Call the flight attendant.
Klingeln Sie nach dem Steward (F.: der Stewardeß)!
KLING-uhln zee naahkh daym "steward" (F.: dayr "stewardess")!

278. Fasten your seat belt.   Anschnallen!
AHN-shnah-luhn!

279. May I smoke?   Darf ich rauchen?
dahrf ikh ROW-khuhn?

280. Will we arrive [on time] [late]?
Kommen wir [pünktlich] [mit Verspätung] an?
KAW-muhn veer [PEWNKT-likh] [mit fer-SHPAY-toong] ahn?

281. Announcement.   Anmeldung (OR: Meldung).
AHN-mel-doong (OR: MEL-doong).

282. Boarding pass.   Einsteigekarte.
IN-shtī-guh-kahr-tuh.

283. Limousine.   Limousine.   *lee-moo-ZEE-nuh.*

TRAIN

284. When does the ticket window [open] [close]?
Wann [öffnet] [schließt] man dèn Fahrkartenschalter?
vahn [URF-nuht] [shleest] mahn dayn FAAHR-kahr-tuhn-shahl-tuhr?

285. When is the next train for [St. Gallen]?
Wann fährt der nächste Zug nach [Sankt Gallen]?
vahn fayrt dayr NAYKH-stuh tsōōk naahkh [zahngkt GAH-luhn]?

286. Is there [an earlier train]?
Gibt es [einen früheren Zug]?
geept es [Ī-nuhn FREW-uh-ruhn tsōōk]?

287. —a later train. —einen späteren Zug.
Ī-nuhn SHPAY-tuh-ruhn tsōōk.

288. —an express train. —einen Fernschnellzug.*
—Ī-nuhn FERN-shnel-tsōōk.

289. —a local train. —einen Personenzug.
—Ī-nuhn per-ZOH-nuhn-tsōōk.

290. From which platform (LIT.: track) does the train leave?
Von welchem Gleis fährt der Zug ab?
fawn VEL-khuhm glīs fayrt dayr tsōōk ahp?

291. Where can I get a timetable?
Wo kann ich einen Fahrplan bekommen?
voh kahn ikh Ī-nuhn FAAHR-plaahn buh-KAW-muhn?

292. Does this train stop at [Linz]?
Hält dieser Zug in [Linz]?
helt DEE-zuhr tsōōk in [lints]?

---

*In Austria and Switzerland: Schnellzug (*SHNEL-tsōōk*).

293. When is there a connecting train (LIT.: **connection) to [Graz]?**
Wann habe ich Anschluß nach [Graz]?
vahn HAAH-buh ikh AHN-shloos naahkh [graahts]?

294. Is there enough time to get off?
Gibt es genug Zeit auszusteigen?
geept es guh-NOOK tsīt OWS-tsoo-shtī-guhn?

295. When do we arrive? Wann kommen wir an?
vahn KAW-muhn veer ahn?

296. Is this seat taken? Ist dieser Platz besetzt?
ist DEE-zuhr plahts buh-ZETST?

297. Am I disturbing you? Störe ich (Sie)?
SHTUR-ruh ikh (zee)?

298. Open the window. Machen Sie das Fenster auf!
MAH-khuhn zee dahs FEN-stuhr owf!

299. Close the door. Machen Sie die Tür zu!
MAH-khuhn zee dee tewr tsoo!

300. Where are we now? Wo sind wir jetzt?
voh zint veer yetst?

301. Is the train on time? Ist der Zug pünktlich?
ist dayr tsook PEWNGKT-likh?

302. How late are we?
Wieviel Verspätung haben wir?
vee-FEEL fer-SHPAY-toong HAAH-buhn veer?

303. Conductor. Schaffner. *SHAHF-nuhr.*

304. Gate. Sperre. *SHPEH-ruh.*

305. Information office (OR: **Information window).**
Auskunftsbüro (OR: Auskunftsschalter).
OWS-koonfts-bew-roh (OR: *OWS-koonfts-shahl-tuhr).*

306. One-way ticket. Einfache Fahrkarte.
ĪN-fah-khuh FAAHR-kahr-tuh.

307. Round-trip ticket. Rückfahrkarte.
REWK-faahr-kahr-tuh.

308. Reserved-seat ticket.* Platzkarte.
PLAHTS-kahr-tuh.

309. Platform ticket. Bahnsteigkarte.
BAAHN-shtīk-kahr-tuh.

310. Railroad (OR: Train) station. Bahnhof.
BAAHN-hohf.

311. Waiting room. Wartesaal. *VAHR-tuh-zaahl.*

312. Sleeping car. Schlafwagen.
SHLAAHF-vaah-guhn.

313. Bedroom compartment. Schlafwagenabteil.
SHLAAHF-vaah-guhn-ahp-tīl.

314. Smoking car. Raucher. *ROW-khuhr.*

315. [First] [Second] call for dinner.
[Erster] [Zweiter] Aufruf zum Essen.
[AYR-stuhr] [TSVĪ-tuhr] OWF-roof tsoom EH-suhn.

316. Dining car. Speisewagen.
SHPĪ-zuh-vaah-guhn.

BUS, SUBWAY, STREETCAR

317. Where does [the streetcar] stop?
Wo hält [die Straßenbahn]?
voh helt [dee STRAAH-suhn-baahn]?

318. How often does [the bus] run?
Wie oft kommt [der Bus]?
vee awft kawmt [dayr boos]?

---

*Your train ticket ("Fahrkarte") allows you only to ride the train. To guarantee yourself a seat, you must buy a "Platzkarte."

319. [Which bus] goes to [Garmisch-Partenkirchen]?
[Welcher Bus] fährt nach [Garmisch-Partenkirchen]?
[VEL-khuhr boos] fayrt naahkh [GAHR-mish-pahr-tuhn-kir-khuhn]?

320. How much is the fare?   Was kostet die Fahrt?
vahs KAWS-tuht dee faahrt?

321. Do you go near [Kärntnerstraße]?
Fahren Sie in die Nähe von [der Kärntnerstraße]?
FAAH-ruhn zee in dee NAY-uh fawn [dayr KERNT-nuhr-shtraah-suh]?

322. I want to get off [at the next stop] [right here].
Ich möchte [an der nächsten Haltestelle] [hier] aussteigen.
ikh MURKH-tuh [ahn dayr NAYKH-stuhn HAHL-tuh-shteh-luh] [heer] OWS-shtī-guhn.

323. Tell me where to get off.
Sagen Sie mir, wo ich aussteigen muß!
ZAAH-guhn zee meer, voh ikh OWS-shtī-guhn moos!

324. Will I have to change (OR: transfer)?
Muß ich umsteigen?
moos ikh OOM-shtī-guhn?

325. Where do we transfer?
Wo müssen wir umsteigen?
voh MEW-suhn veer OOM-shtī-guhn?

326. Driver.   Fahrer.   *FAAH-ruhr.*

327. (A) transfer.   Umsteigekarte.
OOM-shtī-guh-kahr-tuh.

328. Token.   Münze.   *MEWN-tsuh.*

329. (Bus) stop.   Haltestelle.   *HAHL-tuh-shteh-luh.*

330. Where is the subway?
Wo ist die U-Bahn (OR: die Untergrundbahn)?
voh ist dee $\overline{OO}$-baahn (OR: dee OON-tuhr-groont-baahn)?

TAXI

331. Call a taxi for me.
Besorgen Sie mir ein Taxi!
buh-ZAWR-guhn zee meer īn TAH-ksee!

332. Are you free?   Sind Sie frei?   *zint zee frī?*

333. What do you charge [per hour]?
Was berechnen Sie [pro Stunde]?
vahs buh-REKH-nuhn zee [proh SHTOON-duh]?

334. —per kilometer.   —pro Kilometer.
proh kee-loh-MAY-tuhr.

335. —per day.   —pro Tag.   —*proh taahk.*

336. Take me to this address.
Bringen Sie mich zu dieser Adresse!
BRING-uhn zee mikh tsoo DEE-zuhr ah-DREH-suh!

337. How much will the ride cost?
Was kostet die Fahrt?
vahs KAWS-tuht dee faahrt?

338. How long will it take to get there?
Wie lange dauert es hinzufahren?
vee LANG-uh DOW-uhrt es HIN-tsoo-faah-ruhn?

339. Drive (us) around [for one hour].
Fahren Sie [eine Stunde] herum!
FAAH-ruhn zee [Ī-nuh SHTOON-duh] her-OOM!

340. Drive [more carefully] [more slowly].
Fahren Sie [vorsichtiger] [langsamer]!
FAAH-ruhn zee [FOHR-zikh-tih-guhr] [LAHNG-zaah-muhr]!

341. I'm [not] in a great hurry.
Ich bin [nicht] in großer Eile.
ikh bin [nikht] in GROH-suhr Ī-luh.

342. Stop here.
Halten Sie hier!
HAHL-tuhn zee heer!

343. Wait for me here.
Warten Sie hier auf mich!
VAHR-tuhn zee heer owf mĭkh!

344. I'll return in [five minutes].
Ich komme in [fünf Minuten] zurück.
ikh KAW-muh in [fewnf mee-NOO-tuhn] tsoo-REWK.

345. Keep the change.
Der Rest ist für Sie. (OR: Stimmt schon.)
dayr rest ist fewr zee. (OR: shtimt shohn.)

346. The taxi stand.
Der Taxenstand.
dayr TAH-ksuhn-shtahnt.

347. The taxi meter.   Der Taxameter.
dayr tah-ksah-MAY-tuhr.

RENTING AUTOS AND OTHER VEHICLES

348. What kind [of cars] do you have?
Was für [Autos] haben Sie?
vahs fewr [OW-tohs] HAAH-buhn zee?

349. I have an international driver's license.
Ich habe einen internationalen Führerschein.
*ĭkh HAAH-buh Ī-nuhn in-ter-nah-tsee-oh-NAAH-luhn
FEW-ruhr-shĭn.*

350. What does it cost [per day]?
Was kostet es [pro Tag]?
vahs KAWS-tuht es [proh taahk]?

351. How much additional [per kilometer]?
Wieviel mehr [pro Kilometer]?
VEE-feel mayr [proh kee-loh-MAY-tuhr]?

352. Are gas and oil also included in the price?
Sind auch Benzin und Öl im Preis inbegriffen?
*zint owkh ben-TSEEN oont ūrl im prīs IN-buh-grih-
fuhn?*

**353. Does the insurance policy cover [personal
liability]?**
Ist [Haftpflichtversicherung] inbegriffen?
*ist [HAHFT-pflĭkht-fer-zih-k̄huh-roong] IN-buh-grih-
fuhn?*

354. —property damage.
—Sachschadenversicherung.
—ZAHKH-shaah-duhn-fer-zih-k̄huh-roong.

355. —collision. —Kaskoversicherung.
—KAHS-koh-fer-zih-k̄huh-roong.

356. Are the papers in order?
Sind die Papiere in Ordnung?
zint dee pah-PEE-ruh in AWRD-noong?

357. I'm not familiar with this car.
Ich kenne diesen Wagen nicht.
ĭkh KEH-nuh DEE-zuhn VAAH-guhn nĭkht.

358. Explain [this dial] [this mechanism].
Erklären Sie mir [diesen Zeiger] [diesen
Mechanismus]!
*er-KLAY-ruhn zee meer [DEE-zuhn TSĪ-guhr] [DEE-
zuhn meh-khah-NIS-moos]!*

359. Show me how [the heater] operates.
Zeigen Sie mir, wie [die Heizung] funktioniert!
*TSĪ-guhn zee meer, vee [dee HĪ-tsoong] foongk-tsee-oh-
NEERT!*

360. Will someone pick it up at the hotel?
Wird jemand es beim Hotel abholen?
virt YAY-mahnt es bīm hoh-TEL AHP-hoh-luhn?

361. Is the office open all night (LIT.: for 24 hours)?
Ist das Büro vierundzwanzig Stunden offen?
*ist dahs bēw-ROH FEER-oont-tsvahn-tsikh SHTOON-
duhn AW-fuhn?*

362. Bicycle.   Fahrrad.   *FAAHR-raaht.*

363. Motorcycle.   Motorrad.
MOH-tawr-raaht (OR: moh-TOHR-raaht).

364. Motor scooter.   Motorroller.
MOH-tawr-raw-luhr.

365. Horse and wagon.   Gespannfuhrwerk (OR:
Gespann).
guh-SHPAHN-foor-verk (OR: guh-SHPAHN).

366. Moped.   Moped.   *MOH-pet.*

AUTO: DIRECTIONS

367. What's the name of [this city]?
Wie heißt [diese Stadt]?   *vee hīst [DEE-zuh shtaht]?*

368. How far [to the next town]?
Wie weit [bis zur nächsten Stadt]?
vee vīt [bis tsoor NAYKH-stuhn shtaht]?

369. Where does [this road] lead?
Wohin führt [diese Straße]?
voh-HIN fewrt [DEE-zuh SHTRAAH-suh]?

370. Are there road signs?   Gibt es Wegweiser?
geept es VAYK-vī-zuhr?

371. Is the road [paved] [rough]?
Ist die Straße [gepflastert] [uneben (OR: holp(e)rig)]?
ist dee SHTRAAH-suh [guh-PFLAHS-tuhrt] [OON-ay-buhn (OR: HAWLP-(uh)-rikh)]?

372. Show me the easiest way.
Zeigen Sie mir den leichtesten Weg!
TSĪ-guhn zee meer dayn LĪKH-tuhs-tuhn vayk!

373. Show it to me on this road map.
Zeigen Sie es mir auf dieser Straßenkarte!
TSĪ-guhn zee es meer owf DEE-zuhr SHTRAAH-suhn-kahr-tuh!

374. Can I avoid heavy traffic?
Kann ich starken Verkehr umgehen?
kahn ikh SHTAHR-kuhn fer-KAYR oom-GAY-uhn?

375. May I park here [for a while] [overnight]?
Darf ich hier [eine Zeitlang] [übernacht] parken?
dahrf ikh heer [Ī-nuh TSĪT-lahng] [ew-buhr-NAHKHT] PAHR-kuhn?

376. On-ramp.   Einfahrt (OR: Zufahrt).
ĪN-faahrt (OR: TSOO-faahrt).

377. Expressway.   Autobahn.   *OW-toh-baahn.*

378. Fork.   Abzweigung (OR: Gabelung).
AHP-tsvī-goong (OR: GAAH-buh-loong).

379. Intersection.   Kreuzung.   *KROY-tsoong.*

380. Major road.   Hauptstraße.
HOWPT-shtraah-suh.

381. Garage.   Garage.   *gah-RAAH-zhuh.*

382. Auto repair shop.   Reparaturwerkstatt.
reh-pah-rah-TOOR-verk-shtaht.

383. Gas station.   Tankstelle.   *TAHNGK-shteh-luh.*

384. Parking lot (OR: Parking place).   Parkplatz.
PAHRK-plahts.

385. Stop sign.   Stop(p)schild.   *SHTAWP-shilt.*

AUTO: HELP ON THE ROAD

386. My car has broken down.
Mein Wagen (OR: Auto) hat eine Panne.
mīn VAAH-guhn (OR: OW-toh) haht Ī-nuh PAH-nuh.

387. Call a mechanic.   Rufen Sie einen Mechaniker!
ROO-fuhn zee Ī-nuhn may-KHAAH-nee-kuhr!

388. Help me push the car to the side.
Helfen Sie mir, das Auto auf die Seite zu schieben!
*HEL-fuhn zee meer, dahs OW-toh owf dee ZĪ-tuh tsoo
SHEE-buhn!*

389. Can you [push] [tow] me?
Können Sie mich [anschieben] [abschleppen]?
*KUR-nuhn zee mĪkh [AHN-shee-buhn] [AHP-shleh-
puhn]?*

390. May I borrow [a jack]?
Darf ich [einen Wagenheber] borgen?
*dahrf ĪkH [Ī-nuhn VAAH-guhn-hay-buhr] BAWR-
guhn?*

391. Change the tire.   Wechseln Sie den Reifen!
VEK-suhln zee dayn RĪ-fuhn!

392. My car is stuck [in the mud] [in the ditch].
Mein Auto ist [im Schlamm] [im Straßengraben]
   festgefahren.
*mīn OW-toh ist [im shlahm] [im SHTRAAH-suhn-
   graah-buhn] FEST-guh-faah-ruhn.*

393. Drive me to the nearest gas station.
Fahren Sie mich zu der nächsten Tankstelle!
*FAAH-ruhn zee mikh tsoo dayr NAYKH-stuhn
   TAHNGK-shteh-luh!*

AUTO: GAS STATION
AND REPAIR SHOP

394. Give me twenty liters of [regular gasoline].
Geben Sie mir zwanzig Liter [Normalbenzin]!
*GAY-buhn zee meer TSVAHN-tsikh LEE-tuhr [nawr-
   MAAHL-ben-tseen]!*

395. —premium gasoline.   —Superbenzin.
—ZOO-puhr-ben-tseen.

396. —diesel fuel.   —Dieselkraftstoff.
—DEE-zuhl-krahft-shtawf.

397. Fill it up.   Volltanken!   *FAWL-tahng-kuhn!*

398. Check the oil (level).   Prüfen Sie den Ölstand!
PREW-fuhn zee dayn ŪRL-shtahnt!

399. Light oil.   Leichtöl.   *LĪKHT-ūrl.*

400. Heavy oil.   Schweröl.   *SHVAYR-ūrl.*

401. Lubricate the car.   Schmieren Sie das Auto!
SHMEE-ruhn zee dahs OW-toh!

402. Put water in the radiator.
Füllen Sie den Kühler mit Wasser auf!
FEW-luhn zee dayn KEW-luhr mit VAH-suhr owf!

403. Recharge the battery.
Laden Sie die Batterie auf!
LAAH-duhn zee dee bah-tuh-REE owf!

404. Wash the windshield.
Waschen Sie die Windschutzscheibe!
VAH-shuhn zee dee VINT-shoots-shī-buh!

405. Adjust the brakes.
Stellen Sie die Bremsen nach!
SHTEH-luhn zee dee BREM-zuhn naahkh!

406. Check the tire pressure.
Prüfen Sie den Reifendruck!
PREW-fuhn zee dayn RĪ-fuhn-drook!

407. Does it leak? (LIT.: Does the air run out?)
Läuft die Luft aus?   *loyft dee looft ows?*

408. Repair the flat tire.
Reparieren Sie die Reifenpanne (OR: den Reifenschaden)!
reh-pah-REE-ruhn zee dee RĪ-fuhn-pah-nuh (OR: dayn RĪ-fuhn-shaah-duhn)!

409. How long must we wait?
Wie lange müssen wir warten?
vee LAHNG-uh MEW-suhn veer VAHR-tuhn?

410. The motor is overheated.
Der Motor ist überhitzt.
dayr MOH-tawr ist ēw-buhr-HITST.

411. It makes a noise.   Es macht ein Geräusch.
es mahkht īn guh-ROYSH.

412. The headlights don't work.
Die Scheinwerfer funktionieren nicht.
dee SHĪN-ver-fuhr foongk-tsee-oh-NEER-uhn nikht.

413. The car doesn't start.
Der Wagen springt nicht an. __
dayr VAAH-guhn shpringkt nikht ahn.

AUTO: PARTS OF THE CAR (AND AUTO EQUIPMENT)

414. Accelerator.   Gashebel.   *GAAHS-hay-buhl.*

415. Air filter.   Luftfilter.   *LOOFT-fil-tuhr.*

416. Alcohol.   Alkohol.   *AHL-koh-hohl.*

417. Antifreeze.   Frostschutzmittel.
FRAWST-shoots-mih-tuhl.

418. Axle.   Achse.   *AHK-suh.*

419. Bolt.   Schraube.   *SHROW-buh.*

420. Emergency brake.   Notbremse.
NOHT-brem-zuh.

421. Foot brake.   Fußbremse.   *FŌŌS-brem-zuh.*

422. Hand brake.   Handbremse.
HAHNT-brem-zuh.

423. Bumper.   Stoßstange.   *SHTOHS-shtahng-uh.*

424. Carburetor.   Vergaser.   *fer-GAAH-zuhr.*

425. Chassis.   Fahrgestell.   *FAAHR-guh-shtel.*

426. (Automatic) choke.
(Automatische) Starterklappe.
(ow-toh-MAAH-tih-shuh) SHTAHR-tuhr-klah-puh.

427. Clutch.   Kupplung.   *KOOP-loong.*

428. Cylinder. Zylinder. *tsēw-LIN-duhr.*

429. Differential. Ausgleichsgetriebe.
OWS-glīkhs-guh-tree-buh.

430. Directional (OR: **Turn signal**). Biinker.
BLING-kuhr.

431. Door. Tür. *tēwr.*

432. Electrical system. Elektrische Anlage.
ay-LEK-trih-shuh AHN-laah-guh.

433. Engine (OR: **motor**). Motor.
MOH-tawr (OR: *moh-TOHR*).

434. Exhaust pipe. Auspuffrohr. *OWS-poof-rohr.*

435. Exterior. Außenseite. *OW-suhn-zī-tuh.*

436. Fan. Ventilator. *ven-tee-LAAH-tawr.*

437. Fan belt. Ventilatorriemen.
ven-tee-LAAH-tawr-ree-muhn.

438. Fender. Kotflügel. *KOHT-flēw-guhl.*

439. Flashlight. Taschenlampe.
TAH-shuhn-lahm-puh.

440. (Fuel) injection pump. Einspritzpumpe.
ĪN-shprits-poom-puh.

441. Fuel pump. Benzinpumpe.
ben-TSEEN-poom-puh.

442. Fuse. Sicherung. *ZIH-khuh-roong.*

443. Gas tank. Benzintank. *ben-TSEEN-tahngk.*

444. Gear shift. Schalthebel. *SHAHLT-hay-buhl.*

445. [First] gear. [Erster] Gang.
[AYR-stuhr] gahng.

446. Second—. Zweiter—. *TSVĪ-tuhr—.*

447. Third—. Dritter—. *DRIH-tuhr—.*

448. Fourth—. Vierter—. *FEER-tuhr—.*

449. Reverse gear. Rückwärtsgang.
REWK-verts-gahng.

450. Neutral gear. Leerlauf. *LAYR-lowf.*

451. Generator. Generator. *gay-nuh-RAAH-tawr.*

452. Glove compartment. Handschuhfach.
HAHNT-shoo-fahkh.

453. Grease. Schmierfett (OR: Schmiere).
SHMEER-fet (OR: SHMEE-ruh).

454. Hammer. Hammer. *HAH-muhr.*

455. Heater. Heizung. *HĪ-tsoong.*

456. Hood. Haube (OR: Motorhaube).
HOW-buh (OR: MOH-tawr-how-buh).

457. Horn. Hupe. *HOO-puh.*

458. Horsepower. Pferdestärke.
PFAYR-duh-shter-kuh.

459. Ignition key. Zündschlüssel.
TSEWNT-shlew-suhl.

460. Inner tube. Schlauch. *shlowkh.*

461. Instrument panel. Armaturenbrett.
ahr-mah-TOO-ruhn-bret.

462. License plate. Nummernschild.
NOO-muhrn-shilt.

463. Light. Licht. *līkht.*

464. Headlight. Scheinwerfer. *SHĪN-ver-fuhr.*

465. Parking light. Standlicht. *SHTAHNT-līkht.*

466. Brake light. Bremslicht. *BREMS-līkht.*

467. Taillight. Rücklicht (OR: Schlußlicht).
REWK-līkht (OR: SHLOOS-likht).

468. Rear-view mirror.   Innenrückspiegel.
IH-nuhn-rewk-shpee-guhl.

469. Side-view mirror.   Außenspiegel.
OW-suhn-shpee-guhl.

470. Muffler.   Auspufftopf.   *OWS-poof-tawpf.*

471. Nail.   Nagel.   *NAAH-guhl.*

472. Nut.   Mutter (OR: Schraubenmutter).
MOO-tuhr (OR: SHROW-buhn-moo-tuhr).

473. Pedal.   Pedal.   *pay-DAAHL.*

474. Pliers.   Zange.   *TSAHNG-uh.*

475. Radiator.   Kühler.   *KEW-luhr.*

476. Radio.   Radio.   *RAAH-dee-oh.*

477. Rags.   Fetzen.   *FEH-tsuhn.*

478. Rope.   Seil.   *zīl.*

479. Screw.   Schraube.   *SHROW-buh.*

480. Screwdriver.   Schraubenzieher.
SHROW-buhn-tsee-uhr.

481. Automatic shift.
Automatische Schaltung.
ow-toh-MAAH-tih-shuh SHAHL-toong.

482. Hand shift.   Handschaltung.
HAHNT-shahl-toong.

483. Shock absorber.   Stoßdämpfer.
SHTOHS-demp-fuhr.

484. Snow chains.   Schneeketten.
SHNAY-keh-tuhn.

485. Snow tire.   Schneereifen.   *SHNAY-rī-fuhn.*

486. Spark plugs.   Zündkerzen.
TSEWNT-ker-tsuhn.

487. Speedometer. Tachometer.
tah-khoh-MAY-tuhr.

488. Starter. Anlasser. *AHN-lah-suhr.*

489. Steering wheel. Lenkrad (OR: Steuerrad).
LENGK-raaht (OR: SHTOY-uhr-raaht).

490. Tire. Reifen. *RĪ-fuhn.*

491. Spare tire. Reservereifen.
ray-ZER-vuh-rī-fuhn.

492. Tubeless tire. Schlauchloser Reifen.
SHLOWKH-loh-zuhr RĪ-fuhn.

493. Tire pump. Reifenpumpe.
RĪ-fuhn-poom-puh.

494. Tools. Werkzeuge. *VERK-tsoy-guh.*

495. Transmission (automatic).
Automatisches Getriebe.
ow-toh-MAAH-tih-shuhs guh-TREE-buh.

496. Transmission (standard OR manual).
Standardgetriebe.
SHTAHN-dahrt-guh-tree-buh.

497. Trunk. Kofferraum. *KAW-fuhr-rowm.*

498. Valve. Ventil. *ven-TEEL.*

499. Water-cooling system. Wasserkühlung.
VAH-suhr-kēw-loong.

500. Wheel. Rad. *raaht.*

501. Front-wheel drive. Vorderradantrieb.
FOHR-duhr-raaht-ahn-treep.

502. Rear-wheel drive. Hinterradantrieb.
HIN-tuhr-raaht-ahn-treep.

503. Windshield wiper. Scheibenwischer.
SHĪ-buhn-vih-shuhr.

504. Wrench.   Schraubenschlüssel.
SHROW-buhn-shlew-suhl.

MAIL

505. Where is [the post office] [a mailbox]?
Wo ist [die Post (OR: das Postamt)] [ein Briefkasten]?
voh ist [dee pawst (OR: dahs PAWST-ahmt)] [īn
BREEF-kahs-tuhn]?

506. To which window should I go?
An welchen Schalter soll ich gehen?
ahn VEL-k͞huhn SHAHL-tuhr zawl ĭk͞h GAY-uhn?

507. I want to send this [by surface mail].
Ich möchte dies [mit gewöhnlicher Post] schicken.
ĭk͞h MURK͞H-tuh dees [mit guh-VURN-lih-k͞huhr pawst]
SHIH-kuhn.

508. —by air mail.   —per Luftpost.*
—per LOOFT-pawst.

509. —by special delivery.   —durch Eilboten.
—doork͞h ĪL-boh-tuhn.

510. —by registered mail, reply requested.
—eingeschrieben, mit Rückantwort.
—ĪN-guh-shree-buhn, mit REWK-ahnt-vawrt.

511. —by parcel post.   —als Paketpost.
—ahls pah-KAYT-pawst.

512. How much postage do I need [for this postcard]?
Wieviel Porto brauche ich [für diese Postkarte]?
vee-FEEL PAWR-toh BROW-k͞huh ĭk͞h [fewr DEE-zuh
PAWST-kahr-tuh]?

*In Austria: per Flugpost (*per FLŌŌK-pawst*).

513. What's the zip code number for [Frankfurt]?

Was ist die Postleitzahl für [Frankfurt]?

vahs ist dee PAWST-līt-tsaahl fewr [FRAHNGK-foort]?

514. This package contains [printed matter] [fragile material].

Dieses Paket enthält [Drucksachen] [zerbrechliche Sachgüter].

DEE-zuhs pah-KAYT ent-HELT [DROOK-zah-khuhn] [tser-BREKH-lih-khuh ZAHKH-gēw-tuhr].

515. I've already filled out the customs declaration.

Ich habe die Zollerklärung schon ausgefüllt.

ikh HAAH-buh dee TSAWL-er-klay-roong shohn OWS-guh-fewlt.

516. I want to insure this for [25 marks].*

Ich möchte dies für [fünfundzwanzig Mark] versichern.

ikh MURKH-tuh dees fewr [fewnf-oont-TSVAHN-tsikh mahrk] fer-ZIH-khuhrn.

517. Will it still go out today?

Wird es noch heute abgehen?

virt es nawkh HOY-tuh AHP-gay-uhn?

518. Give me ten [90-pfennig]† stamps.

Geben Sie mir zehn Briefmarken [zu neunzig Pfennig]!

GAY-buhn zee meer tsayn BREEF-mahr-kuhn [tsōō NOYN-tsikh PFEH-nikh]!

---

*100 Austrian schillings = Hundert Schilling (*HOON-duhrt SHIH-ling*). 25 Swiss franks = Fünfundzwanzig Franken (*fewnf-oont-TSVAHN-tsikh FRAHNG-kuhn*).

†In Austria: 4-schilling = zu vier Schilling (*tsōō feer SHIH-ling*). In Switzerland: 1-frank = zu einem Franken (*tsōō Ī-nuhm FRAHNG-kuhn*).

519. Do you still have some commemoratives?
Haben Sie noch Sondermarken?
HAAH-buhn zee nawkh ZAWN-duhr-mahr-kuhn?

520. Where can I buy (LIT.: get) a money order?
Wo kann ich eine Postanweisung bekommen?
voh kahn ĭkh Ī-nuh PAWST-ahn-vī-zoong buh-KAW-muhn?

521. Forward my mail to [Salzburg].
Schicken Sie meine Post nach [Salzburg]!
SHIH-kuhn zee MĪ-nuh pawst naahkh [ZAHLTS-boork]!

522. The American Express office will hold my mail.
Das "American Express" Büro wird meine Post
behalten.
dahs "American Express" bēw-ROH virt MĪ-nuh pawst buh-HAHL-tuhn.

523. Where's the counter for general delivery?
Wo ist der Schalter für postlagernde Sendungen?
voh ist dayr SHAHL-tuhr fewr PAWST-laah-guhrn-duh ZEN-doong-uhn?

TELEGRAM

524. I'd like to send [a telegram].
Ich möchte [ein Telegramm] aufgeben.
ikh MURKH-tuh [īn tay-lay-GRAHM] OWF-gay-buhn.

525. —a night letter. —ein Brieftelegramm.
—īn BREEF-tay-lay-grahm.

526. —a cablegram. —ein Überseetelegramm.
—īn EW-buhr-zay-tay-lay-grahm.

527. What is the rate per word?
Was kostet es pro Wort?
vahs KAWS-tuht es proh vawrt?

528. What is the minimum charge?
Was ist die Minimalgebühr?
vahs ist dee mee-nee-MAAHL-guh-bewr?

529. When will an ordinary telegram reach [London]?
Wann wird ein gewöhnliches Telegramm [London]
erreichen?
*vahn virt īn guh-VŪRN-lih-khuhs tay-lay-GRAHM
[LAWN-dawn] ayr-RĪ-khuhn?*

TELEPHONE

530. May I use the telephone?
Darf ich den Fernsprecher (OR: das Telefon) benutzen?
*dahrf ikh dayn FERN-shpreh-khuhr (OR: dahs TAY-lay-
fohn) buh-NOO-tsuhn?*

531. Where (From which telephone) can I dial direct?
Wo kann ich durchwählen?
voh kahn ikh DOORKH-vay-luhn?

532. Will you dial this number for me?
Würden Sie diese Nummer für mich wählen?
*VEWR-duhn zee DEE-zuh NOO-muhr fewr mikh
VAY-luhn?*

**533. Operator (LIT.: Miss), can you connect me with
this number?**
Fräulein, können Sie mich mit dieser Nummer
verbinden?
*FROY-līn, KUR-nuhn zee mikh mit DEE-zuhr NOO-
muhr fer-BIN-duhn?*

534. You have connected me with the wrong number.
Sie haben mich falsch verbunden.
zee HAAH-buhn mikh fahlsh fer-BOON-duhn.

535. We were cut off.
Wir sind unterbrochen worden.
veer zint oon-tuhr-BRAW-khuhn VAWR-duhn.

536. Call me at this number.
Rufen Sie mich unter dieser Nummer an!
ROO-fuhn zee mikh OON-tuhr DEE-zuhr NOO-muhr ahn!

537. My telephone number is [12 34 56].
Ich habe die Nummer [eins zwo* drei vier fünf sechs].
ikh HAAH-buh dee NOO-muhr [īns tsvoh drī feer fewnf zeks].

538. Do you know the area code?
Kennen Sie die Vorwahl?
KEH-nuhn zee dee FOHR-vaahl?

539. How much is a long-distance call to [New York]?
Was kostet ein Ferngespräch nach [New York]?
vahs KAWS-tuht īn FERN-guh-shpraykh naahkh ["New York"]?

540. What is the charge for the first three minutes?
Was kosten die ersten drei Minuten?
vahs KAWS-tuhn dee AYR-stuhn drī mee-NOO-tuhn?

541. I want to reverse the charges (OR: make a collect call).
Ich möchte ein R-Gespräch anmelden.
ikh MURKH-tuh īn AYR-guh-shpraykh AHN-mel-duhn.

---

*On the telephone, use "zwo" (instead of "zwei") for "two" in order to avoid confusion with "drei."

542. I want to place a person-to-person call.
Ich möchte ein Gespräch mit Voranmeldung.
ikh MURKH-tuh īn guh-SHPRAYKH mit FOHR-ahn-mel-doong.

543. They don't answer.
Es meldet sich niemand (OR: Keine Antwort).
es MEL-duht zikh NEE-mahnt (OR: KĪ-nuh AHNT-vawrt).

544. The line is busy. Die Leitung ist besetzt.
dee LĪ-toong ist buh-ZETST.

545. Hello (on the telephone). Hallo. *hah-LOH.*

546. Goodbye (on the telephone) (LIT.: Till [we] hear [each other's voice] again).
Auf Wiederhören. *owf VEE-duhr-hūr-ruhn.*

547. Wrong number (LIT.: I dialed wrong).
Ich habe mich verwählt.
ikh HAAH-buh mikh fer-VAYLT.

548. This is [Anna] speaking.
Hier ist (OR: Hier spricht) [Anna].
heer ist (OR: heer shprikht) [AH-nah].

549. With whom do you wish to speak?
Wen möchten Sie sprechen?
vayn MURKH-tuhn zee SHPREH-khuhn?

550. Hold the line (LIT.: Stay at the phone).
Bleiben Sie am Apparat!
BLĪ-buhn zee ahm ah-pah-RAAHT!

551. Dial again. Wählen Sie noch einmal!
VAY-luhn zee nawkh ĪN-maahl!

552. I can't hear you. Ich kann Sie nicht hören.
ikh kahn zee nikht HUR-ruhn.

553. The connection is poor.
Die Verbindung ist schlecht.
dee fer-BIN-doong ist shlek̲ht.

554. Speak louder.   Sprechen Sie lauter!
SHPREH-k̲huhn zee LOW-tuhr!

555. Have [him] [her] come to the phone.
Lassen Sie [ihn] [sie] zum Telefon kommen!
LAH-suhn zee [een] [zee] tsoom TAY-lay-fohn KAW-muhn!

556. He's not here.   Er ist nicht da.
ayr ist nik̲ht daah.

557. There's a telephone call for you.
Einen Anruf für Sie.
Ī-nuhn AHN-roof fewr zee.

558. Would you take a message?
Würden Sie etwas ausrichten?
VEWR-duhn zee ET-vahs OWS-rik̲h-tuhn?

559. Call me back as soon as possible.
Rufen Sie mich so bald wie möglich zurück!
ROO-fuhn zee mik̲h zoh bahlt vee MURK-lik̲h tsoo-REWK!

560. I'll call back later.   Ich rufe später zurück.
ik̲h ROO-fuh SHPAY-tuhr tsoo-REWK.

561. I'll wait for your call until [six] o'clock.
Ich warte auf Ihren Anruf bis [sechs] Uhr.
ik̲h VAHR-tuh owf EE-ruhn AHN-roof bis [zeks] oor.

HOTEL

562. I'm looking for [a good hotel].
Ich suche [ein gutes Hotel].
Ik̲h ZOO-khuh [īn GOO-tuhs hoh-TEL].

563. —**the best hotel.**   das beste Hotel.
—*dahs BEH-stuh hoh-TEL.*

564. —**an inexpensive hotel.**   —ein billiges Hotel.
—*īn BIH-lih-guhs hoh-TEL.*

565. —**a boarding house (OR: small [private] hotel).**
—eine Pension.
—*Ī-nuh pen-zee-OHN (OR: pang-zee-OHN).*

566. —**an inn.**   —ein Gasthaus.   *īn GAHST-hows.*

567. I [don't] want to be in the center of town.
Ich möchte [nicht] im Stadtzentrum sein.
ikh MURKH-tuh [nikht] im SHTAHT-tsen-troom zīn.

568. I want a quiet location.
Ich möchte es ruhig haben.
ikh MURKH-tuh es ROO-ikh HAAH-buhn.

569. I prefer to be close to [the university].
Ich möchte lieber in der Nähe [der Universität] sein.
ikh MURKH-tuh LEE-buhr in dayr NAY-uh [dayr oo-nee-ver-zee-TAYT] zīn.

570. I have a reservation for tonight.
Ich habe eine Vorbestellung für heute abend.
ikh HAAH-buh Ī-nuh FOHR-buh-shteh-loong fewr HOY-tuh AAH-buhnt.

571. Where is the registration desk?
Wo ist der Empfang?   *voh ist dayr emp-FAHNG?*

572. Fill out the registration form.
Füllen Sie das Anmeldeformular aus!
FEW-luhn zee dahs AHN-mel-duh-fawr-mōō-laahr ows!

573. Sign here.   Unterschreiben Sie hier!
oon-tuhr-SHRĪ-buhn zee heer!

574. Leave your passport.
Lassen Sie Ihren Reisepaß hier!
LAH-suhn zee EE-ruhn RĪ-zuh-pahs heer!

575. You may pick it up later.
Sie können ihn später abholen.
zee KUR-nuhn een SHPAY-tuhr AHP-hoh-luhn.

576. Do you have [a single room]?
Haben Sie [ein Einzelzimmer]?
HAAH-buhn zee [īn ĪN-tsuhl-tsih-muhr]?

577. —a double room. —ein Doppelzimmer.
—īn DAW-puhl-tsih-muhr.

578. —a room with air-conditioning.
—ein Zimmer mit Klimaanlage.
—īn TSIH-muhr mit KLEE-mah-ahn-laah-guh.

579. —a suite. —ein Appartement.
—īn ah-pahr-tuh-MAHNG.

580. —a quiet room. —ein ruhiges Zimmer.
—īn ROO-ih-guhs TSIH-muhr.

581. —an inside room (LIT.: **a room with no window on
the street**).
—ein Zimmer nicht mit Fenster auf die Straße.
*—īn TSIH-muhr nikht mit FEN-stuhr owf dee
SHTRAAH-suh.*

582. —an outside room (LIT.: **a room with a window on
the street**).
—ein Zimmer mit Fenster auf die Straße.
*—īn TSIH-muhr mit FEN-stuhr owf dee SHTRAAH-
suh.*

583. —a room with a pretty view.
—ein Zimmer mit einer schönen Aussicht.
—īn TSIH-muhr mit Ī-nuhr SHUR-nuhn OWS-zikht.

584. I want a room [with a double bed].
Ich möchte ein Zimmer [mit einem Doppelbett].
ikh MURKH-tuh in TSIH-muhr [mit I-nuhm DAW-puhl-bet].

585. —with twin beds. —mit zwei Einzelbetten.
—mit tsvī IN-tsuhl-beh-tuhn.

586. —with a bath. —mit Bad. *—mit baaht.*

587. —with a shower. —mit Dusche.
—mit DOO-shuh.

588. —with running water.
—mit fließendem Wasser.
—mit FLEE-suhn-duhm VAH-suhr.

589. —with hot water. —mit warmem Wasser.
—mit VAHR-muhm VAH-suhr.

590. —with a balcony. —mit Balkon.
—mit bahl-KOHN.

591. —with television. —mit Fernsehen.
—mit FERN-zay-uhn.

592. —with a toilet. —mit WC (OR: Toilette).
—mit vay-TSAY (OR: toh-ah-LEH-tuh).

593. I'll take a room [for one night].
Ich nehme ein Zimmer [für eine Nacht].
ikh NAY-muh in TSIH-muhr [fewr I-nuh nahkht].

594. —for several days. —für mehrere Tage.
—fewr MAY-ruh-ruh TAAH-guh.

595. —for a week or so. —für ungefähr eine Woche.
—fewr OON-guh-fayr I-nuh VAW-khuh.

596. Can I have it [with meals (OR: full board)]?
Kann ich es [mit Vollpension] haben?
kahn ikh es [mit FAWL-pen-zee-ohn) OR: FAWL-pang-zee-ohn)] HAAH-buhn?

597. —without meals.   —ohne Mahlzeiten.
—OH-nuh MAAHL-tsī-tuhn.

598. —with breakfast only.   —nur mit Frühstück.
—nōōr mit FRĒW-shtewk.

599. What is the rate [per night]?
Was kostet es [pro Nacht]?
vahs KAWS-tuht es [proh nahkht]?

600. —per week.   —pro Woche.
—proh VAW-Khuh.

601. —per month.   —pro Monat.
—proh MOH-naht.

602. Are tax and service included?
Sind Steuer und Bedienung inbegriffen?
zint SHTOY-uhr oont buh-DEE-noong IN-buh-grih-fuhn?

603. I'd like to see the room.
Ich möchte mir das Zimmer ansehen.
ikh MURKH-tuh meer dahs TSIH-muhr AHN-zay-uhn.

604. Do you have something [better]?
Haben Sie etwas [Besseres]?
HAAH-buhn zee ET-vahs [BEH-suh-ruhs]?

605. —cheaper.   —Billigeres.   *—BIH-lih-guh-ruhs.*

606. —larger.   —Größeres.   *—GRŪR-suh-ruhs.*

607. —smaller.   —Kleineres.   *—KLĪ-nuh-ruhs.*

608. —on a [lower] [higher] floor.
—auf einem [tieferen] [höheren] Stockwerk.
—owf Ī-nuhm [TEE-fuh-ruhn] [HŪR-uh-ruhn] SHTAWK-verk.

609. —with more light.   —mit mehr Licht.
—mit mayr likht.

610. —with more air. —mit mehr Luft.

—mit mayr looft.

611. —more attractively furnished (LIT.: **with prettier furniture**).

—mit hübscheren Möbeln.

—mit HEWP-shuh-ruhn MUR-buhln.

612. —with a view of the sea.

—mit Ausblick aufs Meer.

—mit OWS-blik owfs mayr.

613. It's too noisy. Es ist zu laut. *es ist tsoo lowt.*

614. This is satisfactory. (LIT.: **good**). Das ist gut. *dahs ist goot.*

615. Is there [an elevator]?

Gibt es [einen Fahrstuhl (OR: Lift, Aufzug)]?

geept es [I-nuhn FAAHR-shtool (OR: lift, OWF-tsook)]?

616. Upstairs. Oben. *OH-buhn.*

617. Downstairs. Unten. *OON-tuhn.*

618. What is my room number?

Was ist meine Zimmernummer?

vahs ist MI-nuh TSIH-nuhr-noo-muhr?

619. Give me my room key.

Geben Sie mir meinen Zimmerschlüssel!

GAY-buhn zee meer MI-nuhn TSIH-muhr-shlew-suhl!

620. Bring my luggage upstairs.

Bringen Sie mein Gepäck nach oben!

BRING-uhn zee min guh-PEK naahk OH-buhn!

621. Tell the chambermaid to get my room ready.

Sagen Sie dem Zimmermädchen, sie soll mein Zimmer aufräumen!

ZAAH-guhn zee daym TSIH-muhr-mayt-khuhn, zee zawl min TSIH-muhr OWF-roy-muhn!

622. Wake me [at eight tomorrow morning].
Wecken Sie mich [morgen früh um acht]!
VEH-kuhn zee mikh [MAWR-guhn frew oom ahkht]!

623. Don't disturb me until then.
Stören Sie mich nicht bis dann!
SHTUR-ruhn zee mikh nikht bis dahn!

624. I want [breakfast] in my room.
Ich möchte [das Frühstück] auf meinem Zimmer.
ikh MURKH-tuh [dahs FREW-shtewk] owf MĪ-nuhm TSIH-muhr.

625. Room service, please.   Zimmerbedienung, bitte!
TSIH-muhr-buh-dee-noong, BIH-tuh!

626. Bring me [some ice cubes].
Bringen Sie mir [Eiswürfel]!
BRING-uhn zee meer [ĪS-vewr-fuhl]!

627. Is there [a letter] for me?
Ist [ein Brief] für mich da?
ist [īn breef] fewr mikh daah?

628. —a message.   —eine Nachricht.
Ī-nuh NAAHKH-rikht.

629. —a parcel.   —ein Paket.   *—īn pah-KAYT.*

630. Send [a chambermaid].
Schicken Sie [ein Zimmermädchen] herauf!
SHIH-kuhn zee [īn TSIH-muhr-mayt-khuhn] heh-ROWF!

631. —a valet.   —einen Hausdiener.
—Ī-nuhn HOWS-dee-nuhr.

632. —a bellhop.   —einen Hotelpagen.
—Ī-nuhn hoh-TEL-paah-zhuhn.

633. —a waiter.   —einen Kellner.
—Ī-nuhn KEL-nuhr.

634. a porter. —einen Hausdiener.
—*Ī-nuhn HOWS-dee-nuhr.*

635. —a messenger. —einen Boten.
—*Ī-nuhn BOH-tuhn.*

636. I'm expecting [a friend].
Ich erwarte [einen Freund (F.: eine Freundin)].
ikh ayr-VAHR-tuh [Ī-nuhn froynt (F.: Ī-nuh FROYN-din)].

637. —a guest (OR: company). —Besuch.
—*buh-ZŌŌKH.*

638. —a telephone call. —einen Anruf.
—*Ī-nuhn AHN-rōōf.*

639. Has anyone called? Hat jemand angerufen?
haht YAY-mahnt AHN-guh-rōō-fuhn?

640. Send [him] [her] up.
Schicken Sie [ihn] [sie] herauf!
SHIH-kuhn zee [een] [zee] heh-ROWF!

641. I won't be here for lunch.
Zu Mittagessen bin ich nicht hier.
tsōō MIH-taahk-eh-suhn bin ikh nikht heer.

642. May I leave [these valuables] in the hotel safe?
Darf ich [diese Kostbarkeiten] im Hoteltresor lassen?
dahrf ikh [DEE-zuh KAWST-baahr-kī-tuhn] im hoh-TEL-tray-zohr LAH-suhn?

643. I'd like to get [my possessions] from the safe.
Ich möchte [meine Habe] aus dem Tresor.
ikh MURKH-tuh [MĪ-nuh HAAH-buh] ows daym tray-ZOHR.

644. When must I check out?
Wann muß ich ausziehen?
vahn moos ikh OWS-tsee-uhn?

645. I'm leaving [at 10 (o'clock)].

Ich reise [um zehn (Uhr)] ab.

ikh RĪ-zuh [oom tsayn ($\overline{oo}$r)] ahp.

646. Make out my bill [as soon as possible].

Machen Sie meine Rechnung [so bald wie möglich] fertig!

MAH-khuhn zee MĪ-nuh REKH-noong [zoh bahlt vee MURK-likh] FER-tikh!

647. Cashier.   Kasse.   *KAH-suh.*

648. Doorman.   Portier.   *pawr-tee-AY.*

CHAMBERMAID

649. The door can't be locked.

Man kann die Tür nicht absperren.

mahn kahn dee tewr nikht AHP-shpeh-ruhn.

650. [The toilet] doesn't work.

[Das Klosett (OR: Die Toilette)] funktioniert nicht.

[dahs kloh-ZET (OR: dee toh-ah-LEH-tuh)] foongk-tsee-oh-NEERT nikht.

651. The room is too [cold] [hot].

Das Zimmer ist zu [kalt] [warm].

dahs TSIH-muhr ist ts$\overline{oo}$ [kahlt] [vahrm].

652. Is this drinking water?   Ist dies Trinkwasser?

ist dees TRINGK-vah-suhr?

653. There is no hot water.

Es kommt kein warmes Wasser.

es kawmt kīn VAHR-muhs VAH-suhr.

654. The sink is clogged.

Das Waschbecken ist verstopft.

dahs VAHSH-beh-kuhn ist fer-SHTAWPFT.

655. The faucet is dripping. Der Wasserhahn tropft.
dayr VAH-suhr-haahn trawpft.

656. Use [insecticide] [pesticide].
Gebrauchen Sie [Insektenvertilgungsmittel]
[Ungeziefervertilgungsmittel]!
guh-BROW-khuhn zee [in-ZEK-tuhn-fer-til-goongs-mih-tuhl] [OON-guh-tsee-fuhr-fer-til-goongs-mih-tuhl]!

657. Wash and iron [this shirt].
Waschen Sie und bügeln Sie [dieses Hemd]!
VAH-shuhn zee oont BEW-guhln zee [DEE-zuhs hemt]!

658. Change the sheets.
Wechseln Sie die Bettwäsche!
VEK-suhln zee dee BET-veh-shuh!

659. Make the bed. Bereiten Sie mein Bett!
buh-RĪ-tuhn zee mīn bet!

660. Bring me [another (an additional) blanket].
Bringen Sie mir [noch eine Decke]!
BRING-uhn zee meer [nawkh Ī-nuh DEH-kuh]!

661. —a bath mat. —einen Badeteppich.
—Ī-nuhn BAAH-duh-teh-pikh.

662. —a bed sheet. —ein Bettlaken.
—īn BET-laah-kuhn.

663. —a candle. —eine Kerze. *—Ī-nuh KER-tsuh.*

664. —some coat hangers. —einige Kleiderbügel.
—Ī-nih-guh KLĪ-duhr-bew-guhl.

665. —a glass. —ein Glas. *īn glaahs.*

666. —a pillow. —ein Kissen. *—īn KIH-suhn.*

667. —a pillowcase. einen Kissenbezug.
—Ī-nuhn KIH-suhn-buh-tsook.

668. —an adapter for electrical appliances.
—einen Zwischenstecker für elektrische Geräte.
—*Ī-nuhn TSVIH-shuhn-shteh-kuhr fewr ay-LEK-trih-shuh guh-RAY-tuh.*

669 —(some) soap. —Seife. *ZĪ-fuh.*

670. —(some) toilet paper. —Toilettenpapier.
—*toh-ah-LEH-tuhn-pah-peer.*

671. —a towel. —ein Handtuch.
īn HAHNT-tōōkh.

672. —a wash cloth. —einen Waschlappen.
—*Ī-nuhn VAHSH-lah-puhn.*

RENTING AN APARTMENT

673. I want to rent [a furnished] [an unfurnished] apartment [with a bathroom].
Ich möchte [eine möblierte] [eine unmöblierte] Wohnung [mit Badezimmer] mieten.
ikh MURKH-tuh [Ī-nuh mur-BLEER-tuh] [Ī-nuh OON-mur-bleer-tuh] VOH-noong [mit BAAH-duh-tsih-muhr] MEE-tuhn.

674. —with two bedrooms.
—mit zwei Schlafzimmern.
—*mit tsvī SHLAAHF-tsih-muhrn.*

675. —with a living room. —mit Wohnzimmer.
—*mit VOHN-tsih-muhr.*

676. —with a dining room. —mit Eßzimmer.
—*mit ES-tsih-muhr.*

677. —with a kitchen. —mit Küche.
—*mit KEW-khuh.*

678. Do you supply [the linen]?
Stellen Sie [die Bettwäsche]?
SHTEH-luhn zee [dee BET-veh-shuh]?

679. —the dishes (OR: china).
—das Geschirr.   —*dahs guh-SHIR.*

680. Do we have to sign a lease for the apartment?
Müssen wir die Wohnung in Pacht* nehmen?
MEW-suhn veer dee VOH-noong in pahkht NAY-muhn?

APARTMENT: USEFUL WORDS

681. Alarm clock.   Wecker.   *VEH-kuhr.*

682. Ashtray. ̄Aschenbecher.
AH-shuhn-beh-k̄huhr.

683. Bathtub.   Badewanne.   *BAAH-duh-vah-nuh.*

684. Bottle opener.   Flaschenöffner.
FLAH-shuhn-urf-nuhr.

685. Broom.   Besen.   *BAY-zuhn.*

686. Can opener.   Büchsenöffner (OR: Dosenöffner).
BEWK-suhn-urf-nuhr (OR: DOH-zuhn-urf-nuhr).

687. Chair.   Stuhl.   *shtool.*

688. Chest of drawers (OR: Bureau).
Kommode.   *kaw-MOH-duh.*

689. Clock.   Uhr.   *ōor.*

690. Cook.   Koch (F.: Köchin).
kawkh (F.: KUR-khin).

*In Austria: in Bestand (*in buh-SHTAHNT*).

691. Cork (stopper).   Korken.*   *KAWR-kuhn.*

692. Corkscrew.   Korkenzieher.
KAWR-kuhn-tsee-uhr.

693. Curtains.   Vorhänge (OR: Gardinen).
FOHR-heng-uh (OR: *gahr-DEE-nuhn*).

694. Cushion.   Kissen.   *KIH-suhn.*

695. Dishwasher.   Abspülmaschine.
AHP-shpewl-mah-shee-nuh.

696. Doorbell.   Klingel.   *KLING-uhl.*

697. Dryer.   Trockner (OR: Trockenapparat).
TRAWK-nuhr (OR: *TRAW-kuhn-ah-pah-raaht*).

698. Fan.   Ventilator.   *ven-tee-LAH-tawr.*

699. Floor.   Fußboden.   *FOOS-boh-duhn.*

700. Hassock.   Kniekissen.   *KNEE-kih-suhn.*

701. Lamp.   Lampe.   *LAHM-puh.*

702. Light bulb.   Glühbirne.   *GLEW-bir-nuh.*

703. Mosquito net.   Moskitonetz.
maws-KEE-toh-nets.

704. Pail.   Eimer.   *Ī-muhr.*

705. Rug.   Teppich.   *TEH-pikh.*

706. Sink (kitchen).   Ausguß.   *OWS-goos.*

707. Switch (light).   Schalter.   *SHAHL-tuhr.*

708. Table.   Tisch.   *tish.*

709. Tablecloth.   Tischtuch.   *TISH-tookh.*

710. Terrace.   Terrasse.   *teh-RAH-suh.*

711. Tray.   Tablett.   *tah-BLET.*

*In Austria: Stoppel (*SHTAW-puhl*), in Switzerland: Zapfen
(*TSAHP-fuhn*).

712. Vase. Vase. *VAAH-zuh.*

713. Venetian blinds. Jalousien.
zhah-lōō-ZEE-uhn.

714. Wardrobe. Schrank. *shrahngk.*

715. Washing machine. Waschmaschine.
VAHSH-mah-shee-nuh.

716. Whisk broom. Handbesen (OR: Handfeger).*
HAHNT-bay-zuhn (OR: *HAHNT-fay-guhr*).

717. Window shades. Rouleaus. *rōō-LOHS.*

CAFÉ AND BAR

718. Bartender, I'd like [a drink].
Barmixer (OR: Barkellner), ich möchte [ein Getränk].
BAR-mik-suhr (OR: *BAR-kel-nuhr*), *ikh MURKH-tuh
[in guh-TRENGK].*

719. —a cocktail. —einen Cocktail.
—Ī-nuhn "cocktail."

720. —a bottle of mineral water [without gas].
—eine Flasche Mineralwasser [ohne Kohlensäure].
*—Ī-nuh FLAH-shuh mee-nay-RAAHL-vah-suhr [OH-
nuh KOH-luhn-zoy-ruh].*

721. —a whiskey [and soda].
—Whisky [mit Selterswasser].
—VIS-kee [mit ZEL-tuhrs-vah-suhr].

722. —a cider. —einen Apfelwein.
—Ī-nuhn AHP-fuhl-vīn.

*In Austria: Bartwisch (*BAHRT-vish*). In Switzerland: Wü-
scherli (*VEW-shuhr-lee*).

723. —a cognac. —einen Kognak.
—*Ī-nuhn KAWN-yahk.*

724. —a brandy. —einen Weinbrand.
—*Ī-nuhn VĪN-brahnt.*

725. —a liqueur (OR: cordial). —ein Likör.
—*īn lih-KURR.*

726. —a gin and tonic. —einen Gin mit Tonic.
—*Ī-nuhn zhin mit TAW-nik.*

727. —rum. —einen Rum. *Ī-nuhn room.*

728. —Scotch whiskey. —einen Scotch.
—*Ī-nuhn "scotch."*

729. —rye whiskey. —einen Whisky.
—*Ī-nuhn VIS-kee.*

730. Bourbon whiskey. —einen Bourbon.
—*Ī-nuhn "bourbon."*

731. —vodka. —einen Wodka.
—*Ī-nuhn VAWT-kah.*

732. —a lemonade. —eine Zitronenlimonade.
—*Ī-nuh tsee-TROH-nuhn-lih-moh-naah-duh.*

733. —a nonalcoholic drink (OR: soft drink).
—ein alkoholfreies Getränk (OR: eine Limonade).
—*īn AHL-koh-hohl-frī-uhs guh-TRENGK (OR: Ī-nuh
lih-moh-NAAH-duh).*

734. —a bottled fruit drink.
—Fruchtsaft in einer Flasche.
—*FROOKHT-zahft in Ī-nuhr FLAH-shuh.*

735. —a bottle of [cola]. —eine Flasche [Cola].
—*Ī-nuh FLAH-shuh [KOH-laah].*

736. —a mug (OR: stein) of beer.
—eine Maß Bier. —*Ī-nuh maahs beer.*

737. —a [light] [dark] beer.
—ein [helles] [dunkles] Bier.
—īn [HEH-luhs] [DOONGK-luhs] beer.

738. —a draft beer. —Bier vom Faß.
—beer fawm faahs.

739. —champagne. —Sekt (OR: Champagner).
—zekt (OR: shahm-PAHN-yuhr).

740. —a glass of sherry. —ein Glas Sherry.
—īn glaahs "sherry."

741. —mulled wine. —Glühwein. *—GLEW̄-vīn.*

742. —[red wine] [white wine].
—[Rotwein] [Weißwein]. *—[ROHT-vīn] [VĪS-vīn].*

743. —rosé. —Rosé. *—"rosé."*

744. Let's have another.
Trinken wir noch eine Runde.
TRING-kuhn veer nawkh Ī-nuh ROON-duh.

745. To your health! (OR: Cheers!)
Zum Wohl! (OR: Prosit!)
tsoom vohl! (OR: PROH-zit!)

RESTAURANT

746. Can you recommend a typical restaurant for [the midday meal] [the evening meal]?
Können Sie ein typisches Restaurant für [das Mittagessen] [das Abendessen] empfehlen?
KUR-nuhn zee īn TEW̄-pih-shuhs reh-stoh-RAAHNG fewr [dahs MIH-taahk-eh-suhn] [dahs AAH-buhnt-eh-suhn] emp-FAY-luhn?

747. Where can one get [breakfast] [sandwiches]?
Wo kann man [Frühstück] [belegte Brote] bekommen?
*voh kahn mahn [FREW-shtewk] [buh-LAYK-tuh
BROH-tuh] buh-KAW-muhn?*

748. Can you recommend [a coffee shop]?
Können Sie [ein Café]* empfehlen?
KUR-nuhn zee [īn kah-FAY] emp-FAY-luhn?

749. —a pastry shop. —eine Konditorei.
—Ī-nuh kawn-dee-toh-RĪ.

750. —a snack bar (OR: "hot dog" stand).
—einen Schnellimbiß (OR: Würstchenstand).
*—Ī-nuhn SHNEL-im-bis (OR: VEWRST-khuhn-
shtahnt).*

**751. Do you serve [lunch]? (LIT.: Can one get [lunch]
here?)**
Kann man hier [Mittagessen] bekommen?
*kahn mahn heer [MIH-taahk-eh-suhn] buh-KAW-
muhn?*

**752. What time is [supper] served? (LIT.: What time is
[supper] eaten?)**
Wann ißt man [das Abendbrot]†?
vahn ist mahn [dahs AAH-buhnt-broht]?

753. A table for [three].
Einen Tisch für [drei Personen].
Ī-nuhn tish fewr [drī per-ZOH-nuhn].

---

*In Austria: ein Kaffeehaus (*īn kah-FAY-hows*). In Switzerland: ein Tea-Room (*īn "tea room"*).

†In central and south Germany: das Abendessen (*dahs AAH-
buhnt-eh-suhn*). In Austria: die Nachtmahl (*dee NAHKHT-
maahl*). In Switzerland: die Znacht (*dee ts-NAHKHT*).

754. Do you serve at this table?
Servieren Sie an diesem Tisch?
zer-VEE-ruhn zee ahn DEE-zuhm tish?

755. I prefer a table [by the window].
Ich hätte gern einen Tisch [am Fenster].
ikh HEH-tuh gern Ī-nuhn tish [ahm FEN-stuhr].

756. —in the corner. —in der Ecke.
—in dayr EH-kuh.

757. —outdoors. —im Freien. *—im FRĪ-uhn.*

758. —indoors. —drinnen. *DRIH-nuhn.*

759. I'd like to wash my hands.
Ich möchte mir die Hände waschen.
ikh MURKH-tuh meer dee HEN-duh VAH-shuhn.

760. [Waiter!] [Waitress!]
[Herr Ober!] [Fräulein!]
[her OH-buhr!] [FROY-līn!]

761. I'd like [an appetizer].
Ich hätte gern [eine Vorspeise].
ikh HEH-tuh gern [Ī-nuh FOHR-shpī-zuh].

762. We want to dine à la carte.
Wir möchten à la carte speisen.
veer MURKH-tuhn "à la carte" SHPĪ-zuhn.

763. We want to dine table d'hôte.
Wir möchten das Menü (OR: das Gedeck) bestellen.
veer MURKH-tuhn dahs meh-NEW (OR: dahs guh-DEK) buh-SHTEH-luhn.

764. We want to eat lightly.
Wir möchten wenig essen.
veer MURKH-tuhn VAY-nikh EH-suhn.

765. What is the speciality of the house?
Was ist die Spezialität des Hauses?
vahs ist dee shpeh-tsee-ah-lee-TAYT des HOW-zuhs?

766. What kind of [fish] do you have?
Was für [Fisch] haben Sie?
vahs fewr [fish] HAAH-buhn zee?

767. Serve us as quickly as you can.
Bedienen Sie uns so schnell wie möglich!
buh-DEE-nuhn zee oons zoh shnel vee MURK-likh!

768. Call the wine steward.
Holen Sie den Weinkellner!
HOH-luhn zee dayn VĪN-kel-nuhr!

769. Bring me [the menu] [the wine list].
Bringen Sie mir [die Speisekarte] [die Weinkarte]!
BRING-uhn zee meer [dee SHPĪ-zuh-kahr-tuh] [dee VĪN-kahr-tuh]!

770. —(tap) water [with] [without] ice.
—Wasser vom Hahn [mit] [ohne] Eis.
—VAH-suhr fawm haahn [mit] [OH-nuh] īs.

771. —a napkin. —eine Serviette.
—Ī-nuh zer-vee-EH-tuh.

772. —bread. —Brot. *—broht.*

773. —butter. —Butter. *—BOO-tuhr.*

774. —a cup. —eine Tasse.* *—Ī-nuh TAH-suh.*

775. —a fork. —eine Gabel.
—Ī-nuh GAAH-buhl.

776. —a glass. —ein Glas. *—īn glaahs.*

777. —a [sharp] knife. —ein [scharfes] Messer.
—īn [SHAHR-fuhs] MEH-suhr.

*In Austria: eine Schale (Ī-nuh SHAAH-luh).

778. —a plate. —einen Teller.
—*Ī-nuhn TEH-luhr.*

779. —a saucer. —eine Untertasse.
—*Ī-nuh OON-tuhr-tah-suh.*

780. —a soup spoon (OR: **tablespoon**).
—einen Suppenlöffel.
—*Ī-nuhn ZOO-puhn-lur-fuhl.*

781. —a teaspoon. —einen Teelöffel.
—*Ī-nuhn TAY-lur-fuhl.*

782. I want something [plain] [without meat].
Ich möchte etwas [Einfaches] [ohne Fleisch].
*ikh MURKH-tuh ET-vahs [ĪN-fah-khuhs] [OH-nuh
flīsh].*

783. Is it canned?
Kommt es aus einer Büchse (OR: Dose)?
kawmt es ows Ī-nuhr BEWK-suh (OR: *DOH-zuh*)?

784. Is it [fatty]? Ist es [fett]? *ist es [fet]?*

785. —fresh. —frisch. *frish.*

786. —frozen. —tiefgefroren.
—*TEEF-guh-froh-ruhn.*

787. —greasy. —fettig. *FEH-tikh.*

788. —lean. —mager. *MAAH-guhr.*

789. —oversalted. —versalzen.
—*fer-ZAHL-tsuhn.*

790. —peppery. —pfeffrig. —*PFEF-rikh.*

791. —spicy. —scharf. —*shahrf.*

792. —very sweet. —sehr süß. —*zayr zēws.*

793. How is it prepared?
Wie wird es zubereitet?
vee virt es TSOO-buh-rī-tuht?

794. Is it [baked]? Ist es [gebacken]?
ist es [guh-BAH-kuhn]?

795. —boiled. —gekocht (OR [for fish]: blau).
—*guh-KAWKHT (OR [for fish]: blow).*

796. —braised. —geschmort. —*guh-SHMAWRT.*

797. —breaded. —paniert. —*pah-NEERT.*

798. —chopped (OR: ground).
—gehackt.* —*guh-HAHKT.*

799. —fried. —(in der Pfanne) gebraten.
—*(in dayr PFAH-nuh) guh-BRAAH-tuhn.*

800. —grilled. —gegrillt. —*guh-GRILT.*

801. —roasted. —gebraten. —*guh-BRAAH-tuhn.*

802. —sauteed. —sautiert. —*zoh-TEERT.*

803. —on a skewer. —an einem Spieß.
—*ahn Ī-nuhm shpees.*

804. —steamed. —gedämpft. —*guh-DEMPFT.*

805. This is [stale (LIT.: not fresh)].
Dies ist [nicht frisch].
dees ist [nikht frish].

806. —too tough. —zu zäh. —*tsōō tsay.*

807. —too dry. —zu trocken.
—*tsōō TRAW-kuhn.*

808. I like the meat [rare].
Ich möchte das Fleisch [rot].
ikh MURKH-tuh dahs flīsh [roht].

809. —medium. —halb durchgebraten.
—*hahlp DOORKH-guh-braah-tuhn.*

810. —well done. —gut durchgebraten.
—*gōōt DOORKH-guh-braah-tuhn.*

---

*In Austria: faschiert (*fah-SHEERT*).

811. This is [undercooked] [burned].
Dies ist [zu wenig gekocht] [angebrannt].
dees ist [tsoo VAY-nikh guh-KAWKHT] [AHN-guh-brahnt].

812. A little [more] [less].
Ein bißchen [mehr] [weniger].
in BIS-khuhn [mayr] [VAY-nih-guhr].

813. Something else.   Etwas anderes.
ET-vahs AHN-duh-ruhs.

814. A small portion.   Eine kleine Portion.
Ī-nuh KLĪ-nuh pawr-tsee-OHN.

815. The next course.   Das nächste Gericht.
dahs NAYKH-stuh guh-RIKHT.

816. I've had enough (LIT.: **I'm full**).
Ich bin satt.   *ikh bin zaht.*

817. This is [not clean] [dirty].
Dies ist [nicht sauber] [schmutzig].
dees ist [nikht ZOW-buhr] [SHMOO-tsikh].

818. This is cold.   Das ist kalt.   *dahs ist kahlt.*

819. I didn't order this.
Ich habe dies nicht bestellt.
ikh HAAH-buh dees nikht buh-SHTELT.

820. You may take this away.
Sie dürfen dies fortnehmen.
zee DEWR-fuhn dees FAWRT-nay-muhn.

821. May I exchange this for [a salad]?
Darf ich dies gegen [einen Salat] tauschen?
dahrf ikh dees GAY-guhn [Ī-nuhn zah-LAAHT] TOW-shuhn?

822. What flavors of [ice cream] do you have?
Was haben Sie an [Eis] da?
vahs HAAH-buhn zee ahn [īs] daah?

823. The check, please.
Die Rechnung, bitte! (OR: Zahlen, bitte!)
dee REKH-noong, BIH-tuh! (OR: TSAAH-luhn, BIH-tuh!)

824. Separate checks.   Getrennte Rechnungen.
guh-TREN-tuh REKH-noong-uhn.

825. Pay at the cashier's desk.
Bezahlen Sie an der Kasse!
buh-TSAAH-luhn zee ahn dayr KAH-suh!

826. Is the tip included?
Ist das Trinkgeld inbegriffen?
ist dahs TRINGK-gelt IN-buh-grih-fuhn?

827. There's a mistake in the bill.
Es ist ein Fehler in der Rechnung.
es ist īn FAY-luhr in dayr REKH-noong.

828. What are these charges (for)?
Was sind diese Beträge?
vahs zint DEE-zuh buh-TRAY-guh?

829. The food and service were excellent.
Das Essen und die Bedienung waren ausgezeichnet.
dahs EH-suhn oont dee buh-DEE-noong VAAH-ruhn OWS-guh-tsīkh-nuht.

830. Enjoy your meal!
Guten Appetit! (OR: Mahlzeit!)
GOO-tuhn ah-pay-TEET! (OR: MAAHL-tsīt!)

FOOD: SEASONINGS

831. Condiments.   Zutaten.   *TSOO-taah-tuhn.*

832. Garlic.   Knoblauch.   *KNOHP-lowkh.*

833. Horseradish. Meerrettich.* *MAYR-reh-tīkh.*

834. Ketchup (OR: Catsup). Tomatenketchup.
toh-MAAH-tuhn-"ketchup."

835. Mayonnaise. Mayonnaise. *mī-aw-NAY-zuh.*

836. [Hot] [mild] mustard. [Scharfer] [Milder] Senf.
[SHAHR-fuhr] [MIL-duhr] zenf.

837. Oil. Öl. *ūrl.*

838. Pepper. Pfeffer. *PFEH-fuhr.*

839. Salt. Salz. *zahlts.*

840. Sauce. Soße. *ZOH-suh.*

841. Sugar. Zucker. *TSOO-kuhr.*

842. Vinegar. Essig. *EH-sĭkh.*

BEVERAGES AND BREAKFAST FOODS

843. I would like (a) [black] [decaffeinated] coffee.
Ich möchte einen [schwarzen] [koffeinfreien] Kaffee.
ĭkh MURKH-tuh Ī-nuhn [SHVAHR-tsuhn] [kaw-fay-EEN-frī-uhn] KAH-fay.†

844. Hot chocolate. Kakao.
kah-KOW (OR: kah-KAAH-oh).

845. Tea with [lemon]. Tee mit [Zitrone].
tay mit [tsee-TROH-nuh].

846. —cream. —Sahne. *—ZAAH-nuh.*

847. —milk. —Milch. *—mĭlkh.*

*In Austria: Kren (*krayn*).

†In Austria: (*kah-FAY*).

848. —artificial sweetener. —Süßstoff.
—*ZEWS-shtawf.*

849. [Iced tea] [Iced coffee].
[Eistee] [Eiskaffee]. *[ĪS-tay] [ĪS-kah-fay].*

850. Grapefruit juice. Pampelmusensaft.
pahm-puhl-MOO-zuhn-zahft.

851. Orange juice. Apfelsinensaft.*
ahp-fuhl-ZEE-nuhn-zahft.

852. Tomato juice. Tomatensaft.
toh-MAAH-tuhn-zahft.

853. Bread. Brot. *broht.*

854. Dark bread. Schwarzbrot.
SHVAHRTS-broht.

855. White bread. Weißbrot. *VĪS-broht.*

856. Pastry. Gebäck. *guh-BEK.*

857. [Soft] [Hard] rolls.
[Weiche] [Harte] Brötchen.†
[VĪ-khuh] [HAHR-tuh] BRURT-khuhn.

858. Toast. Toast. *"toast."*

859. Jam (OR: Marmalade). Marmelade.
mahr-muh-LAAH-duh.

860. Cooked cereal. Brei. *brī.*

861. Dry cereal. Getreideflocken.
guh-TRĪ-duh-flaw-kuhn.

862. Bacon [and eggs]. Speck [mit Eiern].
shpek [mit Ī-uhrn].

---

*In Austria: Orangensaft (*oh-RAHNG-zhuhn-zahft*).

†In south Germany, Austria and parts of G.D.R.: Semmeln
(*ZEH-muhln*). In Switzerland: Weggli (*VEK-lee*).

863. Ham. Schinken. *SHING-kuhn.*

864. Hard-boiled eggs. Hartgekochte Eier.
HAHRT-guh-kawkh-tuh Ī-uhr.

865. Soft-boiled eggs. Weichgekochte Eier.
VĪKH-guh-kawkh-tuh Ī-uhr.

866. Fried eggs. Spiegeleier. *SHPEE-guhl-ī-uhr.*

867. Poached eggs. Verlorene Eier.
fer-LOH-ruh-nuh Ī-uhr.

868. Scrambled eggs. Rühreier. *REWR-ī-uhr.*

869. Omelet. Omelett (in Austria and Switzerland:
Omelette).
awm-(uh)-LET.

SOUPS AND SALADS*

870. Bauernsuppe. *BOW-uhrn-zoo-puh.*
Cabbage and sausage soup.

871. Erbsensuppe. *ERP-suhn-zoo-puh.* Pea soup.

872. Fleischbrühe. *FLĪSH-brew-uh.* Beef broth.

873. Geflügelsalat. *guh-FLEW-guhl-zah-laaht.*
Chicken salad.

874. Gemischter Salat.
guh-MISH-tuhr zah-LAAHT. Mixed salad.

875. Gemüsesuppe. *guh-MEW-zuh-zoo-puh.*
Vegetable soup.

*The following sections include both basic foods and Austrian,
German and Swiss dishes made from them. They are alphabetized
according to the German-language entries to aid you in reading
menus.

876. Grüner Salat.
GREW-nuhr zah-LAAHT.   Green salad.

877. Gurkensalat.
GOOR-kuhn-zah-laaht.   Cucumber salad.

878. Hühnersuppe.   *HEW-nuhr-zoo-puh.*
Chicken soup.

879. Kalte Obstsuppe.   *KAHL-tuh OHPST-zoo-puh.*
Chilled fruit soup.

880. Kaltschale.   *KAHLT-shaah-luh.*
Chilled fruit soup.

881. Kartoffelsalat.
kahr-TAW-fuhl-zah-laaht.   Potato salad.

882. Klare Kraftbrühe.
KLAAH-ruh KRAHFT-brew-uh.   Consommé.

883. Konsommee.   *kohn-saw-MAY.*   Consommé.

884. Kraftbrühe.   *KRAHFT-brew-uh.*   Beef broth.

885. Leberknödelsuppe.
LAY-buhr-knūr-duhl-zoo-puh.
Liver dumpling soup.

886. Linsensuppe.   *LIN-zuhn-zoo-puh.*
Lentil soup.

887. Ochsenschwanzsuppe.
AWK-suhn-shvahnts-zoo-puh.   Oxtail soup.

888. Paradeissuppe. (in Austria)
pah-rah-DĪS-zoo-puh.   Tomato soup.

889. Selleriesalat.   *ZEH-luh-ree-zah-laaht.*
Celery salad.

890. Tomatensalat.
toh-MAAH-tuhn-zah-laaht.   Tomato salad.

891. Tomatensuppe.
toh-MAAH-tuhn-zoo-puh.　　Tomato soup.

892. Zwiebelsuppe.　*TSVEE-buhl-zoo-puh.*
Onion soup.

MEATS AND MEAT DISHES

893. Aufschnitt.　*OWF-shnit.*　　Cold cuts.

894. Beefsteak.　*"beefsteak."*　　Steak.

895. Fleischklößchen.
FLĪSH-klurs-khuhn.　　Meatballs.

896. Gehacktes Rindfleisch.
guh-HAHK-tuhs RINT-flīsh.　　Ground beef.

897. Gehirne.　*guh-HIR-nuh.*　　Brains.

898. Hackbraten.　*HAHK-braah-tuhn.*　　Meatloaf.

899. Hammel.　*HAH-muhl.*　　Mutton.

900. Hase.　*HAAH-zuh.*　　Hare.

901. Herz.　*herts.*　　Heart.

902. Kalbfleisch.　*KAHLP-flīsh.*　　Veal.

903. Kaninchen.　*kah-NEEN-khuhn.*　　Rabbit.

904. Kassler Rippchen.　*KAHS-luhr RIP-khuhn.*
Smoked pork chops.

905. Koteletts.　*koh-tuh-LETS* (OR: *kawt-LETS*).
Chops.

906. Lammfleisch.　*LAHM-flīsh.*　　Lamb.

907. Leber.　*LAY-buhr.*　　Liver.

908. Nieren.　*NEE-ruhn.*　　Kidneys.

909. Rindfleisch.　*RINT-flīsh.*　　Beef.

910. Roast beef. *"roast beef."* Roast beef.

911. Rouladen. *r̄oo-LAAH-duhn.*
Rolled, filled slices of beef.

912. Sauerbraten. *ZOW-uhr-braah-tuhn.*
Braised marinated beef.

913. Schaschlik. *SHAHSH-lik.* Kabobs.

914. Schinken. *SHING-kuhn.* Ham.

915. Schnitzel. *SHNIH-tsuhl.* Cutlets.

916. Schweinefleisch. *SHVĪ-nuh-flīsh.* Pork.

917. Spanferkel. *SHPAAHN-fer-kuhl.*
Roast suckling pig.

918. Wiener Schnitzel. *VEE-nuhr SHNIH-tsuhl.*
Breaded veal cutlet.

919. Wild. *vilt.* Game (OR: Venison).

920. Wurst. *voorst.* Sausage.

POULTRY

921. Backhendl. *BAHK-hen-duhl.*
Breaded fried chicken.

922. Ente. *EN-tuh.* Duck.

923. Gans. *gahns.* Goose.

924. Huhn. *h̄oon.* Chicken.

925. Truthahn. *TR̄OOT-haahn.* Turkey.

926. Pute(r). *P̄OO-tuh(r).* Turkey.

927. Taube. *TOW-buh.* Pigeon.

FISH AND SEAFOOD

928. Aal. *aahl.* Eel.

929. Austern. *OWS-tuhrn.* Oysters.

930. Barsch. *bahrsh.* Bass.

931. Butt. *boot.* Flounder.

932. Eßbare Muscheln.
ES-bah-ruh MOO-shuhln. Clams.

933. Flußkrebs. *FLOOS-krayps.* Crayfish.

934. Flounder. *FLOON-duhr.* Flounder.

935. Forelle. *foh-REH-luh.* Trout.

936. Garnele. *gahr-NAY-luh.* Shrimp.

937. Hecht. *hekht.* Pike.

938. Heilbutt. *HĪL-boot.* Halibut.

939. Hering. *HAY-ring.* Herring.

940. Hummer. *HOO-muhr.* Lobster.

941. Kabeljau. *KAAH-buhl-yow.* Cod.

942. Karpfen. *KAHRP-fuhn.* Carp.

943. Krabbe. *KRAH-buh.* Crab (OR: Shrimp).

944. Krebs. *krayps.* Crab.

945. Lachs. *lahks.* Salmon.

946. Muscheln. *MOO-shuhln.* Mussels.

947. Salm. *zahlm.* Salmon.

948. Sardinen. *zahr-DEE-nuhn.* Sardines.

949. Schellfisch. *SHEL-fish.* Haddock.

950. Schnecken. *SHNEH-kuhn.* Snails.

951. Scholle. *SHAW-luh.* Sole.

952. Schwertfisch. *SHVERT-fish.* Swordfish.

953. Seezunge.   *ZAY-tsoong-uh.*   Sole.

954. Thunfisch.   *TOON-fish.*   Tuna.

VEGETABLES AND STARCHES

955. Artischocken.   *ahr-tee-SHAW-kuhn.*
Artichokes.

956. Aubergine.   *oh-ber-ZHEE-nuh.*   Eggplant.

957. Blaukraut. (in Bavaria)
BLOW-krowt.   Red cabbage.

958. Blumenkohl.   *BLOO-muhn-kohl.*
Cauliflower.

959. Bohnen.   *BOH-nuhn.*   Beans.

960. Bratkartoffeln.   *BRAAHT-kahr-taw-fuhln.*
Fried potatoes.

961. Erbsen.   *ERP-suhn.*   Peas.

962. Erdäpfel. (in Austria)   *AYRT-ep-fuhl.*
Potatoes.

963. Fisolen. (in Austria)   *fee-ZOH-luhn.*
Green beans.

964. Gefüllte Kartoffeln.
guh-FEWL-tuh kahr-TAW-fuhln.   Stuffed potatoes.

965. Gelbe Rüben.   *GEL-buh REW-buhn.*
Carrots.

966. Geröstel.   *guh-RUR-stuhl.*
Hash-brown potatoes.

967. Grüne Bohnen.   *GREW-nuh BOH-nuhn.*
Green beans.

968. Grüne Paprikaschoten.
GRE͞W-nuh PAAHP-ree-kah-shoh-tuhn.
Green peppers.

969. Gurken. *GOOR-kuhn.* Cucumbers.

970. Härdöpfelstock. (in Switzerland)
HERT-urp-fuhl-shtawk. Mashed potatoes.

971. Häuptelsalat. (in Austria)
HOYP-tuhl-zah-laaht. Lettuce.

972. Karfiol. (in Austria)
kahr-fee-OHL.
Cauliflower.

973. Karotten. (in Austria) *kah-RAW-tuhn.*
Carrots.

974. Kartoffelbrei. (in northern Germany and G.D.R.)
kahr-taw-fuhl-BRĪ. Mashed potatoes.

975. Kartoffeln. *kahr-TAW-fuhln.* Potatoes.

976. Kartoffeln in Ofen gebraten.
kahr-TAW-fuhln im OH-fuhn guh-BRAAH-tuhn.
Baked potatoes.

977. Kartoffelpfannkuchen. (in northern and central
  Germany)
kahr-taw-fuhl-PFAHN-ko͞o-khuhn.
Potato pancakes.

978. Kartoffelpuffer. *kahr-taw-fuhl-POO-fuhr.*
Potato pancakes.

979. Kartoffelpüree. *kahr-taw-fuhl-pe͞w-RAY.*
Mashed potatoes.

980. Klöße. *KLU͞R-suh.* Dumplings.

981. Knödel. (in Bavaria and Austria)
KNU͞R-duhl. Dumplings.

982. Kohl.   *kohl.*   Cabbage.

983. Kopfsalat.   *KAWPF-zah-laaht.*   Lettuce.

984. Kraut.   *krowt.*   Cabbage.

985. Lauch. (in southern Germany and Switzerland)
lowkh.   Leek.

986. Limabohnen.   *LEE-mah-boh-nuhn.*
Lima beans.

987. Melanzani. (in Austria)
meh-lahn-TSAHN-nee.   Eggplant.

988. Möhren. (in Austria and central Germany)
MŪR-ruhn.   Carrots.

989. Nudeln.   *NŌŌ-duhln.*   Noodles.

990. Oliven.   *oh-LEE-vuhn.*   Olives.

991. Paradeiser. (in Austria)
pah-rah-DĪ-zuhr.   Tomatoes.

992. Pellkartoffeln.   *PEL-kahr-taw-fuhln.*
Boiled potatoes (in their skins).

993. Petersilie.   *peh-tuhr-ZEE-lee-uh.*   Parsley.

994. Pilze.   *PIL-tsuh.*   Mushrooms.

995. Pommes frites.   *pawm-FREET.*   French fries.

996. Porree.   *PAW-ray.*   Leek.

997. Radieschen.   *rah-DEES-k̄huhn.*   Radish.

998. Reibekuchen. (in the Rhineland)
RĪ-buh-k̄ōō-khuhn.   Potato pancakes.

999. Reiberdatschi. (in Bavaria)
RĪ-buhr-dah-chee.   Potato pancakes.

1000. Reis.   *rīs.*   Rice.

1001. Rettich.   *REH-tĭk̄h.*   Radish.

1002. Rostkartoffeln.
RAWST-kahr-taw-fuhln. Fried potatoes.

1003. Rotkohl. *ROHT-kohl.* Red cabbage.

1004. Rüebli. (in Switzerland)
REW-uhb-lee. Carrots.

1005. Salzkartoffeln. *ZAHLTS-kahr-taw-fuhln.*
Boiled potatoes.

1006. Schwämme. (in Austria)
SHVEH-muh. Mushrooms.

1007. Sellerie. *ZEH-luh-ree.* Celery.

1008. Spaghetti. *shpah-GEH-tee.* Spaghetti.

1009. Spargel. *SHPAHR-guhl.* Asparagus.

1010. Spätzle. *SHPETS-luh.* Short thick noodles.

1011. Spinat. *shpee-NAAHT.* Spinach.

1012. Tätschli. (in Switzerland)
TECH-lee. Potato pancakes.

1013. Tomaten. *toh-MAAH-tuhn.* Tomatoes.

1014. Wachsbohnen. *VAHKS-boh-nuhn.*
Wax (OR: Yellow) beans.

1015. Wurzeln. (in northern Germany)
VOOR-tsuhln. Carrots.

1016. Zwiebeln. *TSVEE-buhln.* Onions.

FRUITS

1017. Ananas. *AH-nah-nahs.* Pineapple.

1018. Apfel. *AHP-fuhl.* Apple.

1019. Apfelsine. *ahp-fuhl-ZEE-nuh.* Orange.

1020. Aprikose. *ahp-ree-KOH-zuh*. Apricot.

1021. Backpflaumen. *BAHK-pflow-muhn*. Prunes.

1022. Banane. *bah-NAAH-nuh*. Banana.

1023. Birne. *BIR-nuh*. Pear.

1024. Datteln. *DAH-tuhln*. Dates.

1025. Erdbeeren. *AYRT-bay-ruhn*. Strawberries.

1026. Feigen. *FĪ-guhn*. Figs.

1027. Himbeeren. *HIM-bay-ruhn*. Raspberries.

1028. Kirschen. *KIR-shuhn*. Cherries.

1029. Marille. (in Austria) *mah-RIH-luh*.
Apricot.

1030. Melone. *may-LOH-nuh*.
Cantaloupe (OR: Melon).

1031. Nüsse. *NEW-suh*. Nuts.

1032. Orange. (in southern Germany, Austria and
Switzerland)
oh-RAHNG-zhuh. Orange.

1033. [Eine halbe] Pampelmuse.
[Ī-nuh HAHL-buh] PAHM-puhl-mōō-zuh (OR: *pahm-
puhl-MOO-zuh*).
[A half] grapefruit.

1034. Pfirsich. *PFIR-zikh*. Peach.

1035. Pflaumen. *PFLOW-muhn*. Plums.

1036. Prünellen. *prew-NEH-luhn*. Prunes.

1037. Quitte. *KVIH-tuh*. Quince.

1038. Trauben. *TROW-buhn*. Grapes.

1039. Zitrone. *tsee-TROH-nuh*. Lemon.

1040. Zwetschgen. (in Bavaria and Austria)
TSVECH-guhn. Plums.

DESSERTS

1041. Apfelstrudel. *AHP-fuhl-shtr$\overline{oo}$-duhl.*
Apple strudel.

1042. Bienenstich. *BEE-nuhn-shtikh.*
Honey and almond cake.

1043. Eierkrem. *Ī-uhr-kraym.* Custard.

1044. Eis. *īs.* Ice cream.

1045. Gebäck. *guh-BEK.* Pastry.

1046. Gugelhupf. *G$\overline{OO}$-guhl-hoopf.*
Bundt cake (OR: Coffee ring).

1047. Kaiserschmarren. *KĪ-zuhr-shmah-ruhn.*
Shredded pancake with raisins.

1048. [Milder] [Scharfer] Käse.
[MIL-duhr] [SHAHR-fuhr] KAY-zuh.
[Mild] [strong] cheese.

1049. Kekse. *KAYK-suh.* Cookies.

1050. Kompott. *kawm-PAWT.* Fruit compote.

1051. Obstkuchen. *OHPST-k$\overline{oo}$-khuhn.* Fruit tart.

1052. Palatschinken. *pah-laaht-SHING-kuhn.*
Filled pancakes (OR: crepes).

1053. Plätzchen. *PLETS-$\overline{kh}$uhn.* Cookies.

1054. Pudding. *POO-ding.* Pudding.

1055. Sachertorte. *ZAH-khuhr-tawr-tuh.*
(Viennese) chocolate layer cake.

1056. Sandkuchen. *ZAHNT-kōō-khuhn.*
Madeira cake.

1057. Schlagobers. (in Austria)
SHLAAHK-oh-buhrs. Whipped cream.

1058. Schlagsahne. *SHLAAHK-zaah-nuh.*
Whipped cream.

1059. Schokolade. *shoh-koh-LAAH-duh.*
Chocolate.

1060. Schokoladeneis. *shoh-koh-LAAH-duhn-īs.*
Chocolate ice cream.

1061. Sorbett. *zawr-BET.* Sherbet.

1062. Streuselkuchen. *SHTROY-zuhl-kōō-khuhn.*
Cake with crumb topping.

1063. Torte. *TAWR-tuh.* Cake.

1064. Vanilleeis. *vah-NIL-yuh-īs.*
Vanilla ice cream.

SIGHTSEEING

1065. I want a licensed guide [who speaks English].
Ich möchte einen offiziellen Führer, [der Englisch
spricht].
*ikh MURKH-tuh Ī-nuhn aw-fee-tsee-EH-luhn FEW-
ruhr, [dayr ENG-lish shprikht].*

**1066. How long will [the excursion] [the guided tour]
take?**
Wie lange dauert [der Ausflug] [die Führung]?
*vee LAHNG-uh DOW-uhrt [dayr OWS-flook] [dee
FEW-roong]?*

1067. Do I need to book in advance?

Muß ich mich im voraus dazu anmelden?

moos ikh mikh im fohr-OWS dah-TSOO AHN-mel-duhn?

1068. Are admission tickets [and a snack] included?

Sind Eintrittskarten [und ein Imbiß] inbegriffen?

zint ĪN-trits-kahr-tuhn [oont īn IM-bis] IN-buh-grih-fuhn?

1069. What is the charge for a trip [to the island]?

Was kostet eine Reise [nach der Insel]?

vahs KAWS-tuht Ī-nuh RĪ-zuh [naahkh dayr IN-zuhl]?

1070. —to the mountains.   —ins Gebirge.

—ins guh-BIR-guh.

1071. —to the sea.   —ans Meer.   *—ahns mayr.*

1072. How much does a tour cost?

Was kostet eine Rundfahrt?

vahs KAWS-tuht Ī-nuh ROONT-faahrt?

1073. Call for me [tomorrow] at my hotel at 8 A.M.

Holen Sie mich [morgen] um acht Uhr früh in meinem Hotel ab!

HOH-luhn zee mikh [MAWR-guhn] oom ahkht ōor frēw in MĪ-nuhm hoh-TEL ahp!

1074. Show me the sights of interest.

Zeigen Sie mir die Sehenswürdigkeiten!

TSĪ-guhn zee meer dee ZAY-uhns-vewr-dikh-kī-tuhn!

1075. What is that building?   Was ist das Gebäude?

vahs ist dahs guh-BOY-duh?

1076. How old is it?   Wie alt ist es?   *vee ahlt ist es?*

1077. Can we go in?   Dürfen wir hinein?

DEWR-fuhn veer hih-NĪN?

1078. I'm interested in [architecture].
Ich interessiere mich für [Architektur].
ikh in-tuh-reh-SEE-ruh mikh fewr [ahr-khee-tek-TOOR].

1079. —archeology. —Archäologie.
—ahr-kheh-ol-loh-GEE.

1080. —sculpture. —Skulptur (OR: Bildhauerei).
—skoolp-TOOR (OR: BILT-how-uhr-ī).

1081. —paintings. —Gemälde.
—guh-MAYL-duh.

1082. —folk art. —Kunstgewerbe.
—KOONST-guh-ver-buh.

1083. —native arts and crafts.
—heimisches Kunstgewerbe.
—HĪ-mih-shuhs KOONST-guh-ver-buh.

1084. —modern art. —moderne Kunst.
—moh-DER-nuh koonst.

1085. I'd like to see [the park].
Ich möchte [den Park] besichtigen.
ikh MURKH-tuh [dayn pahrk] buh-ZIKH-tih-guhn.

1086. —the cathedral. —den Dom. *—dayn dohm.*

1087. —the countryside. —die ländliche Gegend.
—dee LENT-lih-khuh GAY-guhnt.

1088. —the library. —die Bibliothek.
—dee bee-blee-oh-TAYK.

1089. —the ruins. —die Ruinen.
—dee roo-EE-nuhn.

1090. —the castle. —das Schloß. *—dahs shlaws.*

1091. —the palace. —den Palast.
—dayn pah-LAHST.

1092. —the zoo. —den Tiergarten.
—dayn TEER-gahr-tuhn.

1093. Let's take a walk around [the botanical gardens].
Machen wir einen Spaziergang um [den botanischen Garten]!
MAH-khuhn veer Ī-nuhn shpah-TSEER-gahng oom [dayn boh-TAAH-nih-shun GAHR-tuhn]!

1094. Is it a tourist trap? Ist es eine Touristenfalle?
ist es Ī-nuh tōō-RIS-tuhn-fah-luh?

1095. A beautiful view!
Eine wunderschöne Aussicht!
Ī-nuh VOON-duhr-shur-nuh OWS-zikht!

1096. Very interesting! Sehr interessant!
zayr in-tuh-reh-SAHNT!

1097. Magnificent! Herrlich! *HER-likh!*

1098. We're enjoying ourselves.
Wir amüsieren uns gut.
veer ah-mēw-ZEE-ruhn oons gōōt.

1099. I'm bored (LIT.: It is boring to me).
Es ist mir langweilig. *es ist meer LAHNG-vī-likh.*

1100. When does the museum [open] [close]?
Wann wird das Museum [geöffnet] [geschlossen]?
vahn virt dahs mōō-ZAY-oom [guh-URF-net] [guh-SHLAW-suhn]?

1101. Is this the way to the [entrance] [exit]?
Ist dies der Weg zum [Eingang] [Ausgang]?
ist dees dayr vayk tsoom [ĪN-gahng] [OWS-gahng]?

1102. Let's visit the fine arts gallery.
Besuchen wir die Kunstgalerie!
buh-ZŌŌ-khuhn veer dee KOONST-gah-luh-ree!

1103. Let's stay longer. Bleiben wir länger!
BLĪ-buhn veer LENG-uhr!

1104. Let's leave now. Gehen wir jetzt!
GAY-uhn veer yetst!

1105. We must be back by 5 o'clock.
Wir müssen um fünf Uhr zurück sein.
veer MEW-suhn oom fewnf ōōr tsōō-REWK zīn.

1106. If there is time, let's rest a while.
Wenn es genug Zeit gibt, ruhen wir uns ein bißchen
aus!
ven es guh-NŌŌK tsīt geept, RŌŌ-uhn veer oons īn BIS-khuhn ows!

WORSHIP

1107. Altar. Altar. *ahl-TAAHR.*

1108. Catholic church. Katholische Kirche.
kah-TOH-lih-shuh KIR-khuh.

1109. Choral music. Chorgesang.
KOHR-guh-zahng.

1110. Collection plate (LIT.: bag). Klingelbeutel.
KLING-uhl-boy-tuhl.

1111. Communion. Abendmahl (OR: Kommunion).
AAH-buhnt-maahl (OR: kaw-mōō-nee-OHN).

1112. Confession. Beichte. *BĪKH-tuh.*

1113. Contribution. Opfergabe.
AWP-fuhr-gaah-buh.

1114. Mass. Messe. *MEH-suh.*

1115. Minister. Pfarrer. *PFAH-ruhr.*

1116. Prayers. Gebete. *guh-BAY-tuh.*

1117. Prayer book. Gebetbuch.
guh-BAYT-bookh.

1118. Priest. Priester. *PREES-tuhr.*

1119. Protestant church. Evangelische Kirche.
eh-vahng-GAY-lih-shuh KIR-khuh.

1120. Rabbi. Rabbiner. *rah-BEE-nuhr.*

1121. Religious school. Konfessionsschule.
kawn-feh-see-OHNS-shoo-luh.

1122. Sermon. Predigt. *PRAY-dikht.*

1123. Services. Gottesdienste.
GAW-tuhs-deens-tuh.

1124. Sunday school. Sonntagsschule.
ZAWN-taahks-shoo-luh.

1125. Synagogue. Synagoge. *zew-nah-GOH-guh.*

ENTERTAINMENT

1126. Is there [a matinee] today?
Findet heute [eine Matinee] statt?
FIN-duht HOY-tuh [I-nuh mah-tee-NAY] shtaht?

1127. Has [the show] begun?
Hat [die Vorstellung] schon angefangen?
haht [dee FOHR-shteh-loong] shohn AHN-guh-fahng-uhn?

1128. What's playing now? Was wird jetzt gegeben?
vahs virt yetst guh-GAY-buhn?

1129. Do you have any tickets for tonight?
Haben Sie noch Karten für heute abend?
*HAAH-buhn zee nawkh KAHR-tuhn fewr HOY-tuh
AAH-buhnt?*

1130. How much is [a front orchestra seat]?
Wieviel kostet [ein Parkettplatz]?
VEE-feel KAWS-tuht [īn pahr-KET-plahts].

1131. —a back orchestra seat.   —ein Parterreplatz.
—īn pahr-TER-plahts.

1132. —a box.   —eine Loge.   *—Ī-nuh LOH-zhuh.*

1133. —a seat in the dress circle (OR: first balcony).
—ein Platz im ersten Rang.
—īn plahts im AYRS-tuhn rahng.

1134. —a seat in the second balcony.
—ein Platz im zweiten Rang.
—īn plahts im TSVĪ-tuhn rahng.

1135. Not too far from the stage.
Nicht zu weit von der Bühne.
nikht tsoo vīt fawn dayr BEW-nuh.

1136. Here is my stub.
Hier ist mein Kontrollabschnitt (OR: Abschnitt).
heer ist mīn kawn-TRAWL-ahp-shnit (OR: AHP-shnit).

1137. Can I see and hear well from there?
Kahn ich dort gut sehen und hören?
kahn ikh dawrt goot ZAY-uhn oont HUR-uhn?

1138. Follow [the usher].
Folgen Sie [dem Platzanweiser (F.: der
Platzanweiserin)]!
*FAWL-guhn zee [daym PLAHTS-ahn-vī-zuhr (F.: dayr
PLAHTS-ahn-vī-zuh-rin)]!*

1139. Is smoking permitted here?
Darf man hier rauchen?
dahrf mahn heer ROW-khuhn?

1140. How long is the intermission?
Wie lange ist die Pause?
Vee LAHNG-uh ist dee POW-zuh?

1141. When does the performance (OR: show) begin?
Wann fängt die Vorstellung an?
vahn fengkt dee FOHR-shteh-loong ahn?

1142. When does the performance end?
Wann ist die Vorstellung zu Ende?
vahn ist dee FOHR-shteh-loong tsoō EN-duh?

1143. Everyone enjoyed the performance.
Allen hat die Vorstellung gefallen.
AH-luhn haht dee FOHR-shteh-loong guh-FAH-luhn.

1144. Ballet. Ballett. *bah-LET.*

1145. Box office (OR: Ticket window). Theaterkasse.
tay-AAH-tuhr-kah-suh.

1146. Circus. Zirkus. *TSIR-koos.*

1147. Concert. Konzert. *kawn-TSERT.*

1148. Gambling casino. Spielkasino.
SHPEEL-kah-zee-noh.

1149. [The beginning] [The end] of the line.
[Die Spitze] [Das Ende] der Schlange.
[dee SHPIH-tsuh] [dahs EN-duh] dayr SHLAHNG-uh.

1150. Movies. Kino. *KEE-noh.*

1151. Musical comedy.
Musikalisches Lustspiel (OR: Musical).
moō-zee-KAAH-lih-shuhs LOOST-shpeel (OR: "musical").

1152. Nightclub. Nachtlokal (OR: Nachtklub).
NAHKHT-loh-kaahl (OR: NAHKHT-kloop).

1153. Opera. Oper. *OH-puhr.*

1154. Opera glasses. Opernglas.
OH-puhrn-glaahs.

1155. Opera house. Oper (OR: Opernhaus).
OH-puhr (OR: OH-puhrn-hows).

1156. Performance. Vorstellung (OR: Aufführung).
FOHR-shteh-loong (OR: OWF-few-roong).

1157. (Printed) program. Programm.
proh-GRAHM.

1158. Puppet show. Puppenspiel.
POO-puhn-shpeel.

1159. Reserved seat. Reservierter Platz.
ray-zer-VEER-tuhr plahts.

1160. Sporting event.
Sportveranstaltung (OR: Wettkampf).
SHPAWRT-fer-ahn-shtahl-toong (OR: VET-kahmpf).

1161. Standing room. Stehplatz. *SHTAY-plahts.*

1162. Theater. Theater. *tay-AAH-tuhr.*

1163. Variety show. Varieté. *vah-ree-ay-TAY.*

NIGHTCLUB AND DANCING

1164. How much is [the admission charge]?
Wieviel ist [der Eintritt]?
VEE-feel ist [dayr IN-trit]?

1165. —the cover charge. —der Gedeckzuschlag.
—dayr guh-DEK-tsoo-shlaahk.

1166. —the minimum charge. —der Mindestpreis.
—dayr MIN-duhst-prīs.

1167. Is there a floor show (LIT.: performance)?
Gibt es eine Vorstellung?
geept es Ī-nuh FOHR-shteh-loong?

1168. Where can we go to dance?
Wohin können wir tanzen gehen?
voh-HIN KUR-nuhn veer TAHN-tsuhn GAY-uhn?

1169. May I have this dance?
Darf ich um diesen Tanz bitten?
dahrf ikh oom DEE-zuhn tahnts BIH-tuhn?

1170. You dance very well.   Sie tanzen sehr gut.
zee TAHN-tsuhn zayr gōōt.

1171. Will you play [a fox trot]?
Würden Sie [einen Foxtrott] spielen?
VEWR-duhn zee [Ī-nuhn FAWKS-trawt] SHPEE-luhn?

1172. —a rumba.   —einen Rumba.
—Ī-nuhn ROOM-bah.

1173. —a samba.   —einen Samba.
—Ī-nuhn ZAHM-bah.

1174. —a tango.   —einen Tango.
—Ī-nuhn TAHNG-goh.

1175. —a waltz.   —einen Walzer.
—Ī-nuhn VAHL-tsuhr.

1176. —a folk dance.   —einen Volkstanz.
—Ī-nuhn FAWLKS-tahnts.

1177. —rock music.   —Rockmusik.
—RAWK-mōō-zeek.

1178. Discotheque.   Diskothek.   *dis-koh-TAYK.*

SPORTS AND GAMES

1179. We want to play [soccer].
Wir möchten [Fußball] spielen.
veer MURKH-tuhn [FOOS-bahl] SHPEE-luhn.

1180. —basketball. —Korbball (OR: Basketball).
—*KAWRP-bahl (OR: "basketball").*

1181. —cards. —Karten. —*KAHR-tuhn.*

1182. —golf. —Golf. —*gawlf.*

1183. —table tennis (OR: "ping-pong").
—Tischtennis. —*TISH-teh-nis.*

1184. —tennis. —Tennis. —*TEH-nis.*

1185. —volleyball. —Volleyball. —*"volleyball."*

1186. Do you play [chess]? Spielen Sie [Schach]?
SHPEE-luhn zee [shahkh]?

1187. —checkers. —Dame. —*DAAH-muh.*

1188. —bridge. —Bridge. —*"bridge."*

1189. Let's go swimming. Gehen wir schwimmen!
GAY-uhn veer SHVIH-muhn!

1190. Let's go [to the swimming pool].
Gehen wir [zum Schwimmbad]!
GAY-uhn veer tsoom [SHVIM-baaht]!

1191. —to the beach. —an den Strand.
—*ahn dayn shtrahnt.*

1192. —to the horse races. —zum Pferderennen.
—*tsoom PFAYR-duh-reh-nuhn.*

1193. —to the soccer game. —zum Fußballspiel.
—*tsoom FOOS-bahl-shpeel.*

1194. I need [golf equipment].
Ich brauche [Golfausrüstung].
ikh BROW-khuh [GAWLF-ows-rews-toong].

1195. —fishing tackle. —Fischfanggerät.
—*FISH-fahng-guh-rayt.*

1196. —a tennis racket. —einen Tennisschläger.
—*Ī-nuhn TEH-nis-shlay-guhr.*

1197. Can we go [fishing]?   Können wir [angeln]?
KUR-nuhn ver [AHNG-uhln]?

1198. —bicycling.   —radfahren.
—RAAHT-faah-ruhn.

1199. —horseback riding.   —reiten.   *RĪ-tuhn.*

1200. —roller-skating.   —Rollschuh gehen.
—RAWL-shoo GAY-uhn.

1201. —ice-skating.
—Schlittschuh laufen (OR: eislaufen).
—SHLIT-shoo LOW-fuhn (OR: ĪS-low-fuhn).

1202. —sledding.   —schlitten.   *—SHLIH-tuhn.*

1203. —skiing.   —Schi laufen.   *—shee LOW-fuhn.*

HIKING AND CAMPING

1204. How long a walk is it to [the youth hostel]?
Wie lange dauert es zu Fuß zu [der Jugendherberge]?
vee LAHNG-uh DOW-uhrt es tsoo foos tsoo [dayr YŌŌ-guhnt-her-ber-guh]?

1205. Are sanitary facilities available?
Gibt es sanitäre Einrichtung?
geept es zah-nee-TAY-ruh ĪN-rikh-toong?

1206. Campsite.   Campingplatz (OR: Lagerplatz).
KEM-ping-plahts (OR: LAAH-ger-plahts).

1207. Camping equipment.   Campingausrüstung.
KEM-ping-ows-rews-toong.

1208. Camping permit.   Campingerlaubnis.
KEM-ping-er-lowp-nis.

1209. Cooking utensils.   Kochgeräte.
KAWKH-guh-ray-tuh.

1210. Firewood. Brennholz. *BREN-hawlts.*

1211. Footpath. Fußpfad (OR: Gehweg).
FOOS-pfaaht (OR: GAY-vayk).

1212. Garbage receptacle. Abfalleimer.
AHP-fahl-ī-muhr.

1213. Hike. Wanderung. *VAHN-duh-roong.*

1214. Picnic. Picknick. *PIK-nik.*

1215. Shortcut. Abkürzung. *AHP-kewr-tsoong.*

1216. Tent. Zelt. *tselt.*

1217. Thermos. Thermosflasche.
TER-maws-flah-shuh.

1218. Drinking water. Trinkwasser.
TRINGK-vah-suhr.

1219. Forest. Wald. *vahlt.*

1220. Lake. See. *zay.*

1221. Mountain. Berg. *berk.*

1222. River. Fluß. *floos.*

1223. Stream. Bach. *bahkh.*

BANK AND MONEY

**1224. Where can I change foreign money [at the best
rate (LIT.: most advantageously)]?**
Wo kann ich ausländisches Geld [am günstigsten]
wechseln?
*voh kahn ikh OWS-len-dih-shuhs gelt [ahm GEWN-
stikh-stuhn] VEK-suhln?*

1225. What is the exchange rate on the dollar?
Wie steht der Dollar im Kurs?
vee shtayt dayr DAW-lahr im koors?

1226. Will you cash a traveler's check?
Würden Sie einen Reisescheck einlösen?
VEWR-duhn zee Ī-nuhn RĪ-zuh-shek ĪN-lur-zuhn?

1227. I have [a bank draft] [a letter of credit].
Ich habe [einen Bankwechsel] [einen Kreditbrief].
ikh HAAH-buh [Ī-nuhn BAHNGK-vek-suhl]
[Ī-nuhn-kreh-DEET-breef].

1228. I'd like to exchange [twenty] dollars.
Ich möchte [zwanzig] Dollar umwechseln.
ikh MURKH-tuh [TSVAHN-tsikh] DAW-lahr OOM-vek-suhln.

1229. Give me [large bills].
Geben Sie mir [große Scheine]!
GAY-buhn zee meer [GROH-suh SHĪ-nuh]!

1230. —small bills. —kleine Scheine.
—KLĪ-nuh SHĪ-nuh.

1231. —small change. —Kleingeld. *—KLĪN-gelt.*

SHOPPING

1232. Show me [the hat] in the display window.
Zeigen Sie mir [den Hut] im Schaufenster!
TSĪ-guhn zee meer [dayn hoot] im SHOW-fen-stuhr!

1233. I'm just looking around (OR: browsing).
Ich sehe mir nur die Sachen an.
ikh ZAY-uh meer noor dee ZAH-khuhn ahn.

1234. I'll come back later.
Ich komme später zurück.
ikh KAW-muh SHPAY-tuhr tsoo-REWK.

1235. I've been waiting a long time.
Ich warte schon lange.
ikh VAHR-tuh shohn LAHNG-uh.

1236. What brand do you have?
Welche Marke haben Sie?
VEL-khuh MAHR-kuh HAAH-buhn zee?

1237. How much is it [per piece]?
Wieviel kostet [das Stück]?
VEE-feel KAWS-tuht [dahs shtewk]?

1238. —per meter. —das Meter.
—dahs MAY-tuhr.

1239. —per pound. —das Pfund. *—dahs pfoont.*

1240. —per kilo. —das Kilo. *—dahs KEE-loh.*

1241. —per package. —das Paket.
—dahs pah-KAYT.

1242. —per bunch. —das Bund.* *—dahs boont.*

1243. —altogether. —alles zusammen.
—AH-luhs tsoo-ZAH-muhn.

1244. It's [too expensive]. Es ist [zu teuer].
es ist [tsoo TOY-uhr].

1245. —reasonable. —preiswert. *—PRĪS-vert.*

1246. Is that your lowest (LIT.: cheapest) price?
Ist das Ihr billigster Preis?
ist dahs eer BIH-likh-stuhr prīs?

1247. Do you give a discount?
Geben Sie einen Rabatt?
GAY-buhn zee Ī-nuhn rah-BAHT?

---

*(Per) bunch of flowers = der Blumenstrauß (*dayr BLOO-muhn-strows*); (per) bunch of grapes = die Weintraube (*dee VĪN-trow-buh*).

1248. I [don't] like that. ___ Das gefällt mir [nicht].
dahs guh-FELT meer [nikht].

1249. Do you have something [better]?
Haben Sie etwas [Besseres]?
HAAH-buhn zee ET-vahs [BEH-suh-ruhs]?

1250. —cheaper. —Billigeres.
—BIH-lih-guh-ruhs.

1251. —more fashionable. —Modischeres.
—MOH-dih-shuh-ruhs.

1252. —softer. —Weicheres. —*VĪ-khuh-ruhs.*

1253. —stronger. —Solideres.
—zoh-LEE-duh-ruhs.

1254. —heavier. —Schwereres.
—SHVAY-ruh-ruhs.

1255. —lighter (in weight). —Leichteres.
—LĪKH-tuh-ruhs.

1256. —tighter. —Engeres. —*ENG-uh-ruhs.*

1257. —looser. —Loseres. —*LOH-zuh-ruhs.*

1258. —lighter (in color). —Helleres.
—HEH-luh-ruhs.

1259. —darker. —Dunkleres.
—DOONGK-luh-ruhs.

1260. Do you have this in [my size]?
Haben Sie dies in [meiner Größe]?
HAAH-buhn zee dees in [MĪ-nuhr GRUR-suh]?

1261. —a larger size. —einer größeren Nummer.
—Ī-nuhr GRUR-suh-ruhn NOO-muhr.

1262. —a smaller size. —einer kleineren Nummer.
—Ī-nuhr KLĪ-nuh-ruhn NOO-muhr.

1263. May I order it in [another color] [a different style]?

Darf ich es in [einer anderen Farbe] [einem anderen Stil] bestellen?

dahrf ikh es in [Ī-nuhr AHN-duh-ruhn FAHR-buh] [Ī-nuhm AHN-duh-ruhn shteel] buh-SHTEH-luhn?

1264. Where is the dressing (OR: fitting) room?

Wo ist die Umkleidekabine?

voh ist dee OOM-klī-duh-kah-bee-nuh?

1265. May I try it on?   Darf ich es anprobieren?

dahrf ikh es AHN-proh-bee-ruhn?

1266. It doesn't fit.   Es paßt nicht.   *es pahst nikht.*

1267. Too short.   Zu kurz.   *tsoo koorts.*

1268. Too long.   Zu lang.   *tsoo lahng.*

1269. Too big.   Zu groß.   *tsoo grohs.*

1270. Too small.   Zu klein.   *tsoo klīn.*

1271. Take my measurements.

Nehmen Sie mir Maß!   *NAY-muhn zee meer maahs!*

1272. Length.   Länge.   *LENG-uh.*

1273. Width.   Breite (OR: Bahn).

BRĪ-tuh (OR: baahn).

1274. This isn't my size.   Das ist nicht meine Größe.

dahs ist nikht MĪ-nuh GRUR-suh.

1275. Have this ready soon.

Stellen Sie das bald fertig!

SHTEH-luhn zee dahs bahlt FER-tikh!

1276. How long will it take to make the alterations?

Wie lange wird es dauern, um die Änderungen zu machen?

vee LAHNG-uh virt es DOW-uhrn, oom dee EN-duh-roong-uhn tsoo MAH-khuhn?

1277. Does the price include alterations?
Sind Änderungen im Preis inbegriffen?
zint EN-duh-roong-uhn im pris IN-buh-grih-fuhn?

1278. I can't decide.
Ich kann mich nicht entscheiden.
ikh kahn mikh nikht ent-SHĪ-duhn.

1279. I'll wait until it is ready.
Ich warte, bis es fertig ist.
ikh VAHR-tuh, bis es FER-tikh ist.

1280. Wrap this. Packen Sie das ein!
PAH-kuhn zee dahs īn!

1281. Will it [shrink] [break]?
Wird es [eingehen] [zerbrechen]?
virt es [ĪN-gay-uhn] [tser-BREH-khuhn]?

1282. Is it [new]? Ist es [neu]? *ist es [noy]?*

1283. —handmade. —handgemacht.
—HAHNT-guh-mahkht.

1284. —an antique art object.
—ein alter Kunstgegenstand.
—īn AHL-tuhr KOONST-gay-guhn-shtahnt.

1285. —an antique piece of furniture.
—ein antikes Möbelstück.
—īn ahn-TEE-kuhs MŪR-buhl-shtewk.

1286. —a replica. —eine Originalkopie.
—Ī-nuh oh-ree-gee-NAAHL-koh-pee.

1287. —an imitation. —eine Nachbildung.
—Ī-nuh NAAHKH-bil-doong.

1288. —secondhand. —gebraucht.
—guh-BROWKHT.

1289. Where do I pay? Wo zahle ich?
voh TSAAH-luh ikh?

1290. Do I pay the salesclerk?

Zahle ich dem Verkäufer (F.: der Verkäuferin)?

TSAAH-luh ikh [daym fer-KOY-fuhr] [F.: dayr fer-KOY-fuh-rin]?

1291. Will you accept this credit card?

Akzeptieren Sie diese Kreditkarte?

ahk-tsep-TEE-ruhn zee DEE-zuh kreh-DEET-kahr-tuh?

1292. Is this identification acceptable?

Genügt dieser Ausweis?

guh-NEWKT DEE-zuhr OWS-vīs?

1293. Is the reference sufficient?

Genügt das Empfehlungsschreiben?

guh-NEWKT dahs emp-FAY-loongs-shrī-buhn?

1294. Can you send it to [my hotel]?

Können Sie es an [mein Hotel] schicken?

KUR-nuhn zee es ahn [mīn hoh-TEL] SHIH-kuhn?

1295. Can you ship it to [Los Angeles]?

Können Sie es nach [Los Angeles] schicken?

KUR-nuhn zee es naahkh ["Los Angeles"] SHIH-kuhn?

1296. Pack this carefully for export.

Verpacken Sie dies sorgfältig für den Versand ins Ausland!

fer-PAH-kuhn zee dees ZAWRK-fel-tikh fewr dayn fer-ZAHNT ins OWS-lahnt!

1297. Give me [a bill].

Geben Sie mir [eine Rechnung]!

GAY-buhn zee meer [Ī-nuh REKH-noong]!

1298. —a receipt. —eine Quittung.

—Ī-nuh KVIH-toong.

1299. —a credit memo. —eine Gutschriftsanzeige.

—Ī-nuh GOOT-shrifts-ahn-tsī-guh.

1300. I'll pay upon delivery.
Ich bezahle bei der Ablieferung.
ikh buh-TSAAH-luh bī der AHP-lee-fuh-roong.

1301. Is there an additional charge for delivery?
Kommt noch eine Zustellgebühr hinzu?
kawmt nawkh Ī-nuh TSŌŌ-shtel-guh-bēwr hin-TSŌŌ?

1302. I want to return this article.
Ich möchte diese Ware zurückbringen.
ikh MURKH-tuh DEE-zuh VAAH-ruh tsōō-REWK-bring-uhn.

1303. Refund my money.
Geben Sie mir mein Geld zurück!
GAY-buhn zee meer mīn gelt tsōō-REWK!

1304. Exchange this.   Tauschen Sie das!
TOW-shuhn zee dahs!

CLOTHING AND ACCESSORIES

1305. I want to buy [a bathing cap].
Ich möchte [eine Bademütze] kaufen.
ikh MURKH-tuh [Ī-nuh BAAH-duh-mew-tsuh] KOW-fuhn.

1306. —a bathing suit.   —einen Badeanzug.
—Ī-nuhn BAAH-duh-ahn-tsōōk.

1307. —a(n) (elastic) belt.
—einen (elastischen) Gürtel.
—Ī-nuhn (ay-LAHS-tih-shuhn) GEWR-tuhl.

1308. —a blouse.   —eine Bluse.
—Ī-nuh BLŌŌ-zuh.

1309. —boots.   —Stiefel.   *SHTEE-fuhl.*

1310. —a bracelet. —ein Armband.
—*in AHRM-bahnt.*

1311. a brassiere. —einen Büstenhalter.
—*Ī-nuhn BEW-stuhn-hahl-tuhr.*

1312. —briefs. —eine kurze Unterhose.
—*Ī-nuh KOOR-tsuh OON-tuhr-hoh-zuh.*

1313. —a button. —einen Knopf.
—*Ī-nuhn knawpf.*

1314. —a cane (OR: **walking stick**).
—einen Spazierstock.
—*Ī-nuhn shpah-TSEER-shtawk.*

1315. —a cap. —eine Mütze. —*Ī-nuh MEW-tsuh.*

1316. —a coat. —einen Mantel.
—*Ī-nuhn MAHN-tuhl.*

1317. —cufflinks. —Manschettenknöpfe.
—*mahn-SHEH-tuhn-knurp-fuh.*

1318. —a dress. —ein Kleid. —*in klīt.*

1319. —earrings. —Ohrringe. *OHR-ring-uh.*

1320. —a pair of gloves. —ein Paar Handschuhe.
in paahr HAHNT-shōō-uh.

1321. —a handbag (OR: **pocketbook**).
—eine Handtasche. —*Ī-nuh HAHNT-tah-shuh.*

1322. —handkerchiefs. —Taschentücher.
—*TAH-shuhn-tēw-khuhr.*

1323. —a jacket. —eine Jacke.
—*Ī-nuh YAH-kuh.*

1324. —a dinner jacket. —einen Smoking.
—*Ī-nuhn SMOH-king.*

1325. —lingerie. —Damenwäsche.
—*DAAH-muhn-VEH-shuh.*

1326. —a necktie.   —eine Krawatte.*
—Ī-nuh krah-VAH-tuh.

1327. —a nightgown.   —ein Nachthemd.
—īn NAHKHT-hemt.

1328. —pajamas.   —einen Schlafanzug.
—Ī-nuhn SHLAAHF-ahn-tsook.

1329. —panties.   —einen Schlüpfer.
—Ī-nuhn SHLEWP-fuhr.

1330. —panty hose.   —eine Strumpfhose.
—Ī-nuh SHTROOMPF-hoh-zuh.

1331. —a decorative pin.   —eine Schmucknadel.
Ī-nuh SHMOOK-naah-duhl.

1332. —a safety pin.   —eine Sicherheitsnadel.
—Ī-nuh ZIH-khuhr-hīts-naah-duhl.

1333. —a straight pin.   —eine Stecknadel.
—Ī-nuh STEK-naah-duhl.

1334. —a raincoat.   —einen Regenmantel.
—Ī-nuhn RAY-guhn-mahn-tuhl.

1335. —a ribbon.   —ein Band.   —īn bahnt.

1336. —a ring.   —einen Ring.   —Ī-nuhn ring.

1337. —rubbers (OR: galoshes).   —Überschuhe.
—EW-buhr-shoo-uh.

1338. —sandals.   —Sandalen.
—zahn-DAAH-luhn.

1339. —a man's scarf.   —einen Schal.
—Ī-nuhn shaahl.

---

*In northern Germany and G.D.R.:—einen Schlips (—Ī-nuhn shlips). In Bavaria and Austria:—einen Binder OR —einen Selbstbinder (—Ī-nuhn BIN-duhr OR —Ī-nuhn ZELPST-bin-duhr).

1340. —a woman's scarf.   —ein Halstuch.
—*in HAHLS-tōōkh.*

1341. —a shawl.
—ein Umhängetuch (OR: einen Schal).
—*in OOM-heng-uh-tōōkh* (OR: *Ī-nuhn shaahl*).

1342. —a shirt.   —ein Hemd.   —*in hemt.*

1343. —shoelaces.   —Schnürsenkel.*
—*SHNEWR-zeng-kuhl.*

1344. —a pair of shoes.   —ein Paar Schuhe.
—*in paahr SHOO-uh.*

1345. —gym shoes.   —Turnschuhe.
—*TOORN-shōō-uh.*

1346. —walking shorts (for men).
—eine kurze Hose.
—*Ī-nuh KOOR-tsuh HOH-zuh.*

1347. —a pair of slippers.
—ein Paar Hausschuhe (OR: Pantoffeln).
—*in paahr HOWS-shōō-uh* (OR: *pahn-TAW-fuhln*).

1348. —socks.   —Socken.   —*ZAW-kuhn.*

1349. —a skirt.   —einen Rock.   —*Ī-nuhn rawk.*

1350. —a slip.   —einen Unterrock.
—*Ī-nuhn OON-tuhr-rawk.*

1351. —stockings.   —Strümpfe.
—*SHTREWMP-fuh.*

1352. —a man's suit.
—einen Anzug (OR: Herrenanzug).
—*Ī-nuhn AHN-tsōōk* (OR: *HER-ruhn-ahn-tsōōk*).

---

*In Austria: Schuhbänder (*SHOO-ben-duhr*). In southwest
Germany and Switzerland: Schuhbändel (*SHOO-ben-duhl*).

1353. —a woman's suit. —ein Kostüm.
—*īn kaws-TEWM.*

1354. —a sweater (pullover).
—einen Pullover (OR: einen Pulli).
—*Ī-nuhn pool-OH-vuhr* (OR: *Ī-nuhn POO-lee*).

1355. —a T-shirt. —ein T-shirt. —*īn "T-shirt."*

1356. —a pair of trousers. —eine Hose.
—*Ī-nuh HOH-zuh.*

1357. —an umbrella. —einen Regenschirm.
—*Ī-nuhn RAY-guhn-shirm.*

1358. —an undershirt. —ein Unterhemd.
—*īn OON-tuhr-hemt.*

1359. —undershorts. —eine Unterhose.
—*Ī-nuh OON-tuhr-hoh-zuh.*

1360. —underwear. —Unterwäsche.
—*OON-tuhr-veh-shuh.*

1361. —a wallet.
—eine Brieftasche (OR: Geldtasche).
—*Ī-nuh BREEF-tah-shuh* (OR: *GELT-tah-shuh*).

COLORS

1362. Black. Schwarz. *shvahrts.*

1363. Blue. Blau. *blow.*

1364. Light blue. Hellblau. *HEL-blow.*

1365. Dark blue. Dunkelblau.
DOONG-kuhl-blow.

1366. Brown. Braun. *brown.*

1367. Gray. Grau. *grow.*

1368. Green. Grün. *grēwn.*

1369. Olive green. Olivgrün. *oh-LEEF-grēwn.*

1370. Lavender (OR: **Mauve**). Lila. *LEE-lah.*

1371. Orange. Orange. *oh-RAHNG-zhuh.*

1372. Pink. Rosa. *ROH-zah.*

1373. Purple. Purpurrot (OR: Purpurn).
POOR-poor-roht (OR: *POOR-poorn*).

1374. Red. Rot. *roht.*

1375. Tan (OR: **Khaki**).
Bräunlich (OR: Khaki, Staubfarben).
BROYN-likh (OR: *KAAH-kee, SHTOWP-fahr-buhn*).

1376. White. Weiß. *vīs.*

1377. Yellow. Gelb. *gelp.*

MATERIALS

1378. Metal. Metall. *may-TAHL.*

1379. Aluminum. Aluminium.
ah-loo-MEE-nee-oom.

1380. Brass. Messing. *MEH-sing.*

1381. Copper. Kupfer. *KOOP-fuhr.*

1382. Gold. Gold. *gawlt.*

1383. Iron. Eisen. *Ī-zuhn.*

1384. Silver. Silber. *ZIL-buhr.*

1385. (Stainless) Steel. (Rostfreier) Stahl.
(RAWST-frī-uhr) shtaahl.

1386. Tin (OR: **Pewter**). Zinn. *tsin.*

1387. Textiles. Textilien (OR: Textilwaren).
teks-TEE-lee-uhn (OR: *teks-TEEL-vaah-ruhn*).

1388. Corduroy. Kord. *kawrt.*

1389. Cotton. Baumwolle. *BOWM-vaw-luh.*

1390. Denim. Drillich (OR: Jeansstoff).
DRIH-likh (OR: *"JEANS"-shtawf*).

1391. Flame-resistant. Feuerhemmend.
FOY-uhr-heh-muhnt.

1392. Rayon.* Kunstseide. *KOONST-zī-duh.*

1393. Silk. Seide. *ZĪ-duh.*

1394. Synthetic fiber. Kunstfaser.
KOONST-faah-zuhr.

1395. Terrycloth. Frottee. *fraw-TAY.*

1396. Velvet. Samt. *zahmt.*

1397. Wash and wear. Bügelfrei. *BEW-guhl-frī.*

1398. Wool. Wolle. *VAW-luh.*

1399. Wrinkle-resistant. Knitterfrei.
KNIH-tuhr-frī.

1400. Ceramics. Keramik. *keh-RAAH-mik.*

1401. China. Porzellan. *pawr-tseh-LAAHN.*

1402. Crystal. Kristall. *kris-TAHL.*

1403. Fur. Pelz (OR: Fell). *pelts* (OR: *fel*).

1404. Glass. Glas. *glaahs.*

1405. Leather. Leder. *LAY-duhr.*

1406. Plastic. Kunststoff. *KOONST-shtawf.*

1407. Suede. Wildleder. *VILT-lay-duhr.*

1408. Stone. Stein. *shtīn.*

*For dacron, nylon and orlon use the English words and pronunciation.

1409. Wood.   Holz.   *hawlts.*

BOOKSHOP, STATIONER, NEWSDEALER

1410. Do you have [any books] in English?
Haben Sie [irgendwelche Bücher] auf englisch?
HAAH-buhn zee [IR-guhnt-vel-khuh BEW-khuhr] owf ENG-lish?

1411. I'd like (to buy) [playing cards].
Ich möchte [Spielkarten].
ikh MURKH-tuh [SHPEEL-kahr-tuhn].

1412. —a (German-English) dictionary.
—ein (deutsches-englisches) Wörterbuch.
—īn (DOY-chuhs-ENG-lih-shuhs) VUR-tuhr-bōōkh.

1413. —a dozen envelopes.
—ein Dutzend Briefumschläge (OR: Umschläge).*
—īn DOOT-tsuhnt BREEF-oom-shlay-guh (OR: OOM-shlay-guh).

1414. —an eraser.   —einen Radiergummi.
—Ī-nuhn rah-DEER-goo-mee.

1415. —fiction.
—Prosaliteratur (OR: Unterhaltungsliteratur).
—PROH-zah-lih-tuh-rah-tōōr (OR: oon-tuhr-HAHL-toongs-lih-tuh-rah-tōōr).

1416. —folders.   —Aktendeckel (OR: Mappen).
—AHK-tuhn-deh-kuhl (OR: MAH-puhn).

1417. a guidebook.   —einen Reiseführer.
—Ī-nuhn RĪ-zuh-few-ruhr.

---

*In Austria: Kuverts *(kōō-VAYR[S]).*

1418. —ink. —Tinte. —*TIN-tuh.*

1419. —magazines. —Zeitschriften.
—*TSĪT-shrif-tuhn.*

1420. a map. —eine Landkarte.
—*Ī-nuh LAHNT-kahr-tuh.*

1421. a map of the city. —einen Stadtplan.
—*Ī-nuhn SHTAHT-plaahn.*

1422. —a newspaper. —eine Zeitung.
—*Ī-nuh TSĪ-toong.*

1423. —nonfiction. —Sachbücher.
—*ZAHKH-bēw-khuhr.*

1424. —a notebook. —ein Notizheft.
—*īn noh-TEETS-heft.*

1425. airmail stationery. —Luftpostpapier.
—*LOOFT-pawst-pah-peer.*

1426. —carbon paper. —Kohlepapier.
—*KOH-luh-pah-peer.*

1427. —notepaper. —Briefpapier.
—*BREEF-pah-peer.*

1428. —a writing pad. —einen Schreibblock.
—*Ī-nuhn SHRĪP-blawk.*

1429. —a ballpoint pen.
—einen Kugelschreiber (OR: einen Kuli).
—*Ī-nuhn KŌŌ-guhl-shrī-buhr* (OR: *Ī-nuhn KŌŌ-lee*).

1430. —a felt-tip pen. —einen Filzschreiber.
—*Ī-nuhn FILTS-shrī-buhr.*

1431. a fountain pen. —eine Füllfeder.
—*Ī-nuh FEWL-fay-duhr.*

1432. —a pencil. —einen Bleistift.
—*Ī-nuhn BLĪ-shtift.*

1433. —masking tape. —Abdeckband. —*AHP-dek-bahnt.*

1434. —transparent tape. —durchsichtigen Klebestreifen. —*DOORKH-zikh-tih-guhn KLAY-buh-shtrī-fuhn.*

1435. —string.* —Schnur. —*shnoor.*

1436. —a typewriter. —eine Schreibmaschine. —*Ī-nuh SHRĪP-mah-shee-nuh.*

1437. typewriter ribbon. —ein Farbband. —*īn FAHRP-bahnt.*

1438. —wrapping paper. —Packpapier. —*PAHK-pah-peer.*

PHARMACY

1439. Is there [a pharmacy] here where they understand English?
Gibt es hier [eine Apotheke], wo man Englisch versteht?
geept es heer [Ī-nuh ah-poh-TAY-kuh], voh mahn ENG-lish fer-SHTAYT?

1440. May I speak to [a male clerk] [a female clerk]?
Darf ich mit [einem Verkäufer] [einer Verkäuferin] sprechen?
dahrf ikh mit [Ī-nuhm fer-KOY-fuhr] [Ī-nuhr fer-KOY-fuh-rin] SHPREH-khuhn?

---

*In northern Germany and G.D.R.: Bindfaden (*BINT-faah-duhn*). In the Rhineland: Kordel (*KAWR-duhl*). In Austria: Spagat (*shpah-GAAHT*).

1441. Can you fill this prescription [immediately]?
Können Sie dieses Rezept [sofort] anfertigen?
*KUR-nuhn zee DEE-zuhs reh-TSEPT [zoh-FAWRT]
AHN-fer-tih-guhn?*

1442. Is it [mild] [safe]?
Ist es [mild] [unschädlich]?
ist es [milt] [OON-shayt-likh]?

1443. Antibiotic. Antibiotikum.
ahn-tee-bee-OH-tee-koom.

1444. Sleeping pills. Schlaftabletten.
SHLAAHF-tah-bleh-tuhn.

1445. Poison. Gift. *gift.*

1446. Tranquilizers. Beruhigungstabletten.
buh-ROO-ih-goongs-tah-bleh-tuhn.

1447. Warning. Warnung. *VAHR-noong.*

1448. Take as directed (LIT.: Following instructions of
the physician).
Nach Vorschrift des Arztes.
naahk FOHR-shrift des AAHRTS-tuhs.

1449. Not to be taken internally.
Nicht innerlich anzuwenden.
nikht IH-nuhr-likh AHN-tsoo-ven-duhn.

1450. For external use only.
Nur äußerlich anzuwenden.
noor OY-suhr-likh AHN-tsoo-ven-duhn.

DRUGSTORE ITEMS

1451. Adhesive bandage. Schnellverband
(OR: Pflaster).
SHNEL-fer-bahnt (OR: *PFLAHS-tuhr*).

1452. Adhesive tape. Heftpflaster.
HEFT-pflahs-tuhr.

1453. Alcohol. Alkohol. *AHL-koh-hohl.*

1454. Antiseptic. Antiseptikum.
ahn-tee-ZEP-tee-koom.

1455. Antiseptic cream. Wundsalbe.
VOONT-zahl-buh.

1456. Aspirin (OR: **Analgesic**). Aspirin.
ahs-pee-REEN.

1457. Bandages. Verbandzeug (OR: Verbandstoff).
fer-BAHNT-tsoyk (OR: *fer-BAHNT-shtawf*).

1458. Bath oil. Badeöl. *BAAH-duh-ūrl.*

1459. Bath salts. Badesalz. *BAAH-duh-zahlts.*

1460. Bicarbonate of soda.
Doppelkohlensäures Natrium (OR: Natron).
DAW-puhlt-koh-luhn-zoy-ruhs NAAH-tree-oom (OR:
NAAH-trawn).

1461. Boric acid. Borsäure. *BOHR-zoy-ruh.*

1462. Chewing gum. Kaugummi. *KOW-goo-mee.*

1463. Cleaning fluid.
Reinigungsmittel als Flüssigkeit.
RĪ-nih-goongs-mih-tuhl ahls FLEW-sikh-kīt.

1464. Cold cream (OR: **Cleansing cream**).
Reinigungscreme. *RĪ-nih-goongs-kraym.*

1465. Cologne. Kölnischwasser.
KURL-nish-vah-suhr.

1466. Comb. Kamm. *kahm.*

1467. (Powder) compact. Kompaktpuderdose. *kawm-PAHKT-p$\overline{oo}$-duhr-doh-zuh.*

1468. Contraceptive. Verhütungsmittel. *fer-H$\overline{EW}$-toongs-mih-tuhl.*

1469. Corn pads. Hühneraugenpflaster. *H$\overline{EW}$-nuhr-ow-guhn-pflahs-tuhr.*

1470. Cotton (absorbent). Watte. *VAH-tuh.*

1471. Cough drops. Hustenbonbons. *H$\overline{OO}$S-tuhn-bawng-bawng.*

1472. Cough syrup. Hustensaft. *H$\overline{OO}$S-tuhn-zahft.*

1473. Deodorant. Desodorierendes Mittel. *des-oh-doh-REE-ruhn-duhs MIH-tuhl.*

1474. Depilatory. Enthaarungsmittel. *ent-HAAH-roongs-mih-tuhl.*

1475. Disinfectant. Desinfektionsmittel. *des-in-fek-tsee-OHNS-mih-tuhl.*

1476. Ear plugs. Ohrenstöpsel. *OH-ruhn-shturp-suhl.*

1477. Enema bag. Klistiertüte. *klis-TEER-t$\overline{ew}$-tuh.*

1478. Epsom salts. Epsomer Bittersalz. *EP-suh-muhr BIH-tuhr-zahlts.*

1479. Eye cup.__ Augenbecher. *OW-guhn-beh-khur.*

1480. Eye wash. Augenwasser. *OW-guhn-vah-suhr.*

1481. Facial tissues. Papiertaschentücher. *pah-PEER-tah-shuhn-t$\overline{ew}$-khuhr.*

1482. Gauze (bandage).
Verbandmull (OR: Mullbinde).
fer-BAHNT-mool (OR: *MOOL-bin-duh*).

1483. Hairbrush.   Haarbürste.
HAAHR-bewrs-tuh.

1484. Hair clip.   Haarclip.   *HAAHR-"clip."*

1485. Hair net.   Haarnetz.   *HAAHR-nets.*

1486. Hairpins.   Haarnadeln.
HAAHR-naah-duhln.

1487. Hair spray.   Haarspray.   *HAAHR-shpray.*

1488. Hand lotion.   Handcreme.   *HAHNT-kraym.*

1489. Hot-water bottle.   Warmflasche.
VAHRM-flah-shuh.

1490. Ice bag.   Eisbeutel.   *ĪS-boy-tuhl.*

1491. Iodine.   Jod.   *yoht.*

1492. Laxative (mild).   (Mildes) Abführmittel.
(MIL-duhs) AHP-fewr-mih-tuhl.

1493. Lipstick.   Lippenstift.   *LIH-puhn-shtift.*

1494. Medicine dropper.   Pipette.   *pee-PEH-tuh.*

1495. Mirror.   Spiegel.   *SHPEE-guhl.*

1496. Mouthwash.   Mundwasser.
MOONT-vah-suhr.

1497. Nail file.   Nagelfeile.   *NAAH-guhl-fī-luh.*

1498. Nailpolish.   Nagellack.   *NAAH-guhl-lahk.*

1499. Nail polish remover.   Nagellackentferner.
NAAH-guhl-lahk-ent-fer-nuhr.

1500. Nose drops.   Nasentropfen.
NAAH-zuhn-trawp-fuhn.

1501. Ointment (OR: Salve).   Salbe.   *ZAHL-buh.*

1502. Peroxide (OR: Hydrogen peroxide).
Superoxyd (OR: Wasserstoffsuperoxyd).
ZOO-puhr-awk-sewt (OR: VAH-suhr-shtawf-zoo-puhr-awk-sewt).

1503. Powder. Puder. *POO-duhr.*

1504. Face powder. Gesichtspuder.
guh-ZIKHTS-poo-duhr.

1505. Foot powder. Fußpuder.
FOOS-poo-duhr.

1506. Talcum powder. Talkumpuder.
TAHL-koom-poo-duhr.

1507. Powder puff. Puderquaste.
POO-duhr-kvahs-tuh.

1508. Straight razor. Rasiermesser.
rah-ZEER-meh-suhr.

1509. Electric razor (OR: Electric shaver).
Elektrischer Rasierapparat.
ay-LEK-trih-shuhr rah-ZEER-ah-pah-raaht.

1510. Safety razor. Rasierapparat.
rah-ZEER-ah-pah-raaht.

1511. Razor blades. Rasierklingen.
rah-ZEER-kling-uhn.

1512. Rouge. Rouge. *roozh.*

1513. Sanitary napkins. Binden. *BIN-duhn.*

1514. <u>Sedative</u>. Beruhigungsmittel.
buh-ROO-ih-goongs-mih-tuhl.

1515. Setting lotion. Haarfestiger.
HAAHR-fes-tih-guhr.

1516. Shampoo. Shampoo (OR: Haarwaschmittel).
shem-POO (OR: HAAHR-vahsh-mih-tuhl).

1517. Shaving brush.   Rasierpinsel.
rah-ZEER-pin-zuhl.

1518. Shaving cream (brushless).   Rasierkreme.
rah-ZEER-kraym.

1519. Shaving lotion.   Rasierwasser.
rah-ZEER-vah-suhr.

1520. Shower cap.   Bademütze zum Duschen.
BAAH-duh-mew-tsuh tsoom DOO-shuhn.

1521. Smelling salts.   Riechsalz.   *REEKH-zahlts.*

1522. Sponge.   Schwamm.   *shvahm.*

1523. Sunburn ointment.   Sonnenbrandsalbe.
ZAW-nuhn-brahnt-zahl-buh.

1524. Sunglasses.   Sonnenbrille.
ZAW-nuhn-brih-luh.

1525. Suntan oil (OR: lotion).   Sonnenöl.
ZAW-nuhn-ūrl.

1526. Syringe.   Spritze.   *SHPRIH-tsuh.*

1527. Tampons.   Tampons.   *TAHM-pawns.*

1528. Thermometer (Celsius).   Thermometer
(Celsius).
ter-moh-MAY-tuhr (TSEL-zee-oos).

1529. Toothbrush.   Zahnbürste.
TSAAHN-bewr-stuh.

1530. Toothpaste.   Zahnpasta.   *TSAAHN-pahs-tah.*

1531. Toothpowder.   Zahnpulver.
TSAAHN-pool-fuhr.

1532. Tweezers.   Pinzette.   *pin-TSEH-tuh.*

1533. Vaseline.   Vaselin (OR: Vaseline).
vah-zay-LEEN (OR: vah-zay-LEE-nuh).

1534. Vitamins.   Vitaminen.   *vee-tah-MEE-nuhn.*

CAMERA SHOP AND PHOTOGRAPHY

1535. I want a roll of film [for this camera].
Ich möchte einen Film [für diesen Apparat].
ikh MURKH-tuh I-nuhn film [fewr DEE-zuhn ah-pah-RAAHT].

1536. Do you have [color film]?
Haben Sie [Farbfilm]?
HAAH-buhn zee [FAHRP-film]?

1537. —black-and-white film.
—Schwarz-Weiß-Film. —*shvahrts-VĪS-film.*

1538. —movie film. —Schmalfilm (OR: Super acht Film).
—*SHMAAHL-film* (OR: *ZOO-puhr ahkht film*).

1539. What is the charge [for developing a roll]?
Was berechnen Sie [für das Entwickeln eines Films]?
vahs buh-REKH-nuhn zee [fewr dahs ent-VIH-kuhln I-nuhs films]?

1540. —for an enlargement.
—für eine Vergrößerung.
—*fewr I-nuh fer-GRUR-suh-roong.*

1541. —for one print. —für einen Abzug.
—*fewr I-nuhn AHP-tsook.*

1542. May I take a photo of you?
Darf ich Sie aufnehmen?
dahrf ikh zee OWF-nay-muhn?

1543. Would you take a photo of [me] [us]?
Würden Sie [mich] [uns] aufnehmen?
VEWR-duhn zee [mikh] [oons] OWF-nay-muhn?

1544. Color print. Farbabzug. *FAHRP-ahp-tsook.*

1545. Flash cubes. Blitzwürfel. *BLITS-vewr-fuhl.*

1546. Electronic flash. Elektronischer Blitz. *ay-lek-TROH-nih-shuhr blits.*

1547. Lens. Objektiv. *awp-yek-TEEF.*

1548. Negative. Negativ. *nay-gah-TEEF.*

1549. Slide (OR: **Transparency**). Diapositiv. *dee-ah-poh-zee-TEEF.*

1550. Tripod. Stativ. *ïn shtah-TEEF.*

See also "Repairs and Adjustments," p. 126.

GIFT AND SOUVENIR LIST

1551. Basket. Korb. *kawrp.*

1552. Box of chocolates. Schachtel Pralinen. *SHAHKH-tuhl prah-LEE-nuhn.*

1553. Doll. Puppe. *POO-puh.*

1554. Embroidery. Stickerei. *shtih-kuh-RĪ.*

1555. Handicrafts. Kunsthandwerk. *KOONST-hahnt-verk.*

1556. Jewelry. Schmuck. *shmook.*

1557. Lace. Spitze. *SPIH-tsuh.*

1558. Needlework. Näherei. *nay-uh-RĪ.*

1559. Penknife. (Kleines) Taschenmesser. *(KLĪ-nuhs) TAH-shuhn-meh-suhr.*

1560. Perfume. Parfüm. *pahr-FEWM.*

1561. Phonograph records. Schallplatten.
SHAHL-plah-tuhn.

1562. Pottery. Töpferwaren.
TURP-fuhr-vaah-ruhn.

1563. Precious stone. Edelstein. *AY-duhl-shtīn.*

1564. Print (graphic).
Graphischer Abzug (OR: Stich).
GRAH-fih-shuhr AHP-tsōōk (OR: shtikh).

1565. Reproduction (of a painting, etc.).
Nachbildung. *NAAHKH-bil-doong.*

1566. Souvenir. Andenken. *AHN-den-kuhn.*

1567. Toys. Spielwaren. *SHPEEL-vaah-ruhn.*

TOBACCO STORE

1568. Where is the nearest tobacco store?
Wo ist der nächste Tabakladen?*
voh ist dayr NAYKH-stuh TAAH-bahk-laah-duhn?

1569. I want some cigars.
Ich möchte ein paar Zigarren.
ikh MURKH-tuh īn paahr tsee-GAH-ruhn.

1570. What brands of American cigarettes [with menthol] do you have?
Welche Marken von amerikanischen Zigaretten [mit Menthol] haben Sie?
VEL-khuh MAHR-kuhn fawn ah-may-ree-KAAH-nih-shuhn tsee-gah-REH-tuhn [mit men-TOHL] HAAH-buhn zee?

*In Austria: die nächste Trafik (*dee NAYKH-stuh trah-FIK*).

1571. One pack of king-size [filter-tip] cigarettes.
Eine Schachtel extra lang Zigaretten [mit Filter].
Ī-nuh SHAHKH-tuhl "extra" lahng tsee-gah-REH-tuhn [mit FIL-tuhr].

1572. I need [a lighter].
Ich brauche [ein Feuerzeug].
ikh BROW-khuh [īn FOY-uhr-tsoyk].

1573. —lighter fluid.   —Feuerzeugbenzin.
—FOY-uhr-tsoyk-ben-tseen.

1574. —a flint.   —einen Feuerstein.
—Ī-nuhn FOY-uhr-shtīn.

1575. —matches.   —Streichhölzer.*
—SHTRĪKH-hurl-tsuhr.

1576. —a pipe.   —eine Pfeife.   *—Ī-nuh PFĪ-fuh.*

1577. —pipe cleaners.   —Pfeifenreiniger.
—PFĪ-fuhn-rī-nih-guhr.

1578. —pipe tobacco.   —Pfeifentabak.
—PFĪ-fuhn-taah-bahk.

1579. —a tobacco pouch.   —einen Tabakbeutel.
—Ī-nuhn TAAH-bahk-boy-tuhl.

LAUNDRY AND DRY CLEANING

1580. Where can I have my laundry washed?
Wo kann ich meine Wäsche waschen lassen?
voh kahn ikh MĪ-nuh VEH-shuh VAH-shuhn LAH-suhn?

*In Bavaria and Austria: —Zündhölzl (—*TSEWNT-hawl-zuhl*). (In Switzerland: —Zündhölzli (—*TSEWNT-hurlts-lee*).

1581. Is there a dry-cleaning service near here?
Gibt es eine chemische Reinigungsanstalt in der Nähe?
geept es Ī-nuh K͞HAY-mih-shuh RĪ-nih-goongs-ahn-shtahlt in dayr NAY-uh?

1582. Wash this blouse in [hot water].
Waschen Sie diese Bluse in [heißem Wasser]!
VAH-shuhn zee DEE-zuh BLŌŌ-zuh in [HĪ-suhm VAH-suhr]!

1583. —warm water. —warmem Wasser.
—VAHR-muhm VAH-suhr.

1584. —lukewarm water. —lauwarmem Wasser.
—LOW-vahr-muhm VAH-suhr.

1585. —cold water. —kaltem Wasser.
—KAHL-tuhm VAH-suhr.

1586. No starch. Ohne Stärkemehl (OR: Stärke).
OH-nuh SHTER-kuh-mayl (OR: SHTER-kuh).

1587. Remove the stain [from this shirt].
Entfernen Sie den Fleck [von diesem Hemd]!
ent-FER-nuhn zee dayn flek [fawn DEE-zuhm hemt]!

1588. Press [the trousers]. Bügeln Sie [die Hose]!
BEW-guhln zee [dee HOH-zuh]!

1589. Starch [the collar]. Stärken Sie [den Kragen]!
SHTER-kuhn zee [dayn KRAAH-guhn]!

1590. Dry-clean [this coat].
Reinigen Sie [diesen Mantel] (chemisch)!
RĪ-nih-guhn zee [DEE-zuhn MAHN-tuhl] (K͞HAY-mish)!

1591. [The belt] is missing. [Der Gürtel] fehlt.
[dayr GEWR-tuhl] faylt.

1592. Sew on [this button].
Nähen Sie [diesen Knopf] an!
NAY-uhn zee [DEE-zuhn knawpf] ahn!

REPAIRS AND ADJUSTMENTS

1593. This doesn't work.   Dies funktioniert nicht.
dees foongk-tsee-oh-NEERT nikht.

1594. This watch (OR: clock) is [fast] [slow].
Diese Uhr geht [vor] [nach].
DEE-zuh oor gayt [fohr] [naahkh].

1595. [My glasses] are broken.
[Meine Brille] ist kaputt.
[MĪ-nuh BRIH-luh] ist kah-POOT.

1596. It is torn.   Es ist zerrissen.
es ist tser-RIH-suhn.

1597. Where can I get it repaired?
Wo kann ich es reparieren lassen?
voh kahn ikh es ray-pah-REE-ruhn LAH-suhn?

1598. Repair (OR: fix) [this lock].
Reparieren Sie [dieses Schloß]!
ray-pah-REE-ruhn zee [DEE-zuhs shlaws]!

1599. —the sole.   —die Sohle.   —*dee ZOH-luh.*

1600. —the heel.   —den Absatz.
—*dayn AHP-zahts.*

1601. —the uppers.   —das Oberleder.
—*dahs OH-buhr-lay-duhr.*

1602. —the strap.   —den Riemen.
—*dayn REE-muhn.*

1603. Adjust [this hearing aid].
Regulieren Sie [diesen Hörapparat]! __
ray-goo-LEE-ruhn zee [DEE-zuhn HURR-ah-pah-raaht]!

1604. Lengthen [this skirt].
Machen Sie [diesen Rock] länger!
MAH-k̄huhn zee [DEE-zuhn rawk] LENG-uhr!

1605. Shorten [the sleeves].
Machen Sie [die Ärmel] kürzer!
MAH-k̄huhn zee [dee ER-muhl] KEWR-tsuhr!

1606. Replace [the lining].
Ersetzen Sie [die Fütterung]!
er-ZEH-tsuhn zee [dee FEW-tuh-roong]!

1607. Mend [the pocket].   Flicken Sie [die Tasche]!
FLIH-kuhn zee [dee TAH-shuh]!

1608. Fasten it together.   Binden Sie es zusammen!
BIN-duhn zee es tsōō-ZAH-muhn!

1609. Clean [the mechanism].
Reinigen Sie [den Mechanismus]!
RĪ-nih-guhn zee [dayn may-k̄hah-NIS-moos]!

1610. Lubricate [the spring].
Ölen (OR: Schmieren) Sie [die Feder (OR: die Sprungfeder)]!
ŪR-luhn (OR: SHMEE-ruhn) zee [dee FAY-duhr (OR: dee SHPROONG-fay-duhr)]!

1611. Needle.   Nadel.   *NAAH-duhl.*

1612. Scissors.   Schere.   *SHAY-ruh.*

1613. Thimble.   Fingerhut.   *FING-uhr-hōōt.*

1614. Thread.   Garn (OR: Zwirn).
gahrn (OR: tsvirn).

BARBER SHOP

1615. A haircut, please. Haarschneiden, bitte.
HAAHR-shnī-duhn, BIH-tuh.

1616. Just a trim. Nur ausputzen.
nōōr OWS-poo-tsuhn.

1617. (A) shave. Rasieren. *rah-ZEE-ruhn.*

1618. Shoeshine. Schuhe putzen.
SHOO-uh POO-tsuhn.

1619. Don't cut (LIT.: Don't take away) much off [the top].
Nehmen sie [oben] nicht viel weg!
NAY-muhn zee [OH-buhn] nĭkht feel vek!

1620. —the sides. —an den Seiten.
—ahn dayn ZĪ-tuhn.

1621. —the neck. —im Nacken. *—im NAH-kuhn.*

1622. I want to keep (LIT.: wear) my hair long.
Ich möchte lange Haare tragen.
ĭkh MURKH-tuh LAHNG-uh HAAH-ruh TRAAH-guhn.

1623. I part my hair (LIT.: I wear the part) [on this side].
Ich trage den Scheitel [auf dieser Seite].
ĭkh TRAAH-guh dayn SHĪ-tuhl [owf DEE-zuhr ZĪ-tuh].

1624. —on the other side. —auf der anderen Seite.
—owf dayr AHN-duh-ruhn ZĪ-tuh.

1625. —in the middle. —in der Mitte.
—in dayr MIH-tuh.

1626. [No] hair tonic. [Kein] Haarwasser.
[kīn] HAAHR-vah-suhr.

1627. Trim [my mustache].
Stutzen Sie mir [den Schnurrbart]!
SHTOO-tsuhn zee meer [dayn SHNOOR-bahrt]!

1628. —my eyebrows. —die Augenbrauen.
—dee OW-guhn-brow-uhn.

1629. —my beard. —den Bart. *—dayn bahrt.*

1630. —my sideburns. —die Koteletten.
—dee koh-tuh-LEH-tuhn (OR: *kawt-LEH-tuhn*).

BEAUTY PARLOR

1631. May I make an appointment for [Monday afternoon]?
Darf ich mich für [Montag nachmittag] anmelden?
dahrf ikh mikh fewr [MOHN-taahk NAAHKH-mih-taahk] AHN-mel-duhn?

1632. Comb my hair. Kämmen Sie mir die Haare!
KEH-muhn zee meer dee HAAH-ruh!

1633. Wash my hair. Waschen Sie mir die Haare!
VAH-shuhn zee meer dee HAAH-ruh!

1634. Shampoo and set. Waschen und legen.
VAH-shuhn oont LAY-guhn.

1635. Blow-dry my hair.
Trocknen Sie die Haare mit dem Föhn!
TRAWK-nuhn zee dee HAAH-ruh mit daym furn!

1636. Not too short. Nicht zu kurz.
nikht tsoo koorts.

1637. This style. Diese Frisur.
DEE-zuh free-ZOOR.

1638. Dye my hair [in this shade].
Färben Sie mir die Haare [diese Farbe]!
FER-buhn zee meer dee HAAH-ruh [DEE-zuh FAHR-buh]!

1639. Clean and set this wig.
Waschen Sie und legen Sie diese Perücke!
VAH-shuhn zee oont LAY-guhn zee DEE-zuh peh-REW-kuh!

1640. Curl. Locke. *LAW-kuh.*

1641. Facial. Gesichtsmassage.
guh-ZIKHTS-mah-saah-zhuh.

1642. Hairpiece. Haarteil. *HAAHR-tīl.*

1643. Color rinse. Farbspülung.
FAHRP-shpew-loong.

1644. Manicure. Maniküre. *mah-nee-KEW-ruh.*

1645. Massage. Massage. *mah-SAAH-zhuh.*

1646. Permanent wave. Dauerwelle.
DOW-uhr-veh-luh.

STORES AND SERVICES

1647. Antique shop. Antiquitätenhandlung.
ahn-tee-kvee-TAY-tuhn-hahnt-loong.

1648. Art gallery. Kunstgalerie.
KOONST-gah-luh-ree.

1649. Artist's materials. Zeichenmaterialien.
TSĪ-khuhn-mah-tay-ree-aah-lee-uhn.

1650. Auto repairs. Autoreparaturwerkstatt.
OW-toh-ray-pah-rah-tōōr-verk-shtaht.

1651. Bakery. Bäckerei. *beh-kuh-RĪ.*

1652. Bank. Bank. *bahngk.*

1653. Bar. Bar. *baahr.*

1654. Barber (OR: Men's hairdresser).
Friseur (OR: Herrenfriseur).
free-ZURR (OR: HEH-ruhn-free-zurr).

1655. Butcher shop. Metzgerei.* *mets-guh-RĪ.*

1656. Candy shop. Süßwarengeschäft.
ZEWS-vaah-ruhn-guh-sheft.

1657. Car rental. Autovermietung.
OW-toh-fer-mee-toong.

1658. Checkroom. Garderobe.
gahr-duh-ROH-buh.

1659. Clothing store. Kleidergeschäft.
KLĪ-duhr-guh-sheft.

1660. Children's clothing store.
Kinderkleidergeschäft.
KIN-duhr-klī-duhr-guh-sheft.

1661. Ladies' clothing. Damenkleidergeschäft.
DAAH-muhn-klī-duhr-guh-sheft.

1662. Men's clothing store. Herrenkleidergeschäft.
HEH-ruhn-klī-duhr-guh-sheft.

1663. Cosmetics. Kosmetikartikel.
kaws-MAY-tik-ahr-tee-kuhl.

1664. Dance studio. Tanzschule.
TAHNTS-shoo-luh.

1665. Delicatessen. Feinkostgeschäft.
FĪN-kawst-guh-sheft.

---

*In northern Germany: Schlachterei (*shlahkh-tuh-RĪ*). In
G.D.R.: Fleischerei (*flī-shuh-RĪ*). In Austria: Fleischhauerei
(*flīsh-how-uh-RĪ*).

1666. Dentist.   Zahnarzt.   *TSAAHN-aahrtst.*

1667. Department store.   Kaufhaus.   *KOWF-hows.*

1668. Dressmaker.
Modistin (OR: Damenschneiderin).
moh-DIS-tin (OR: *DAH-muhn-shnī-duh-rin*).

1669. Drugstore (OR: **Pharmacy**).
Drogerie (OR: Apotheke).
droh-guh-REE (OR: *ah-poh-TAY-kuh*).

1670. Electrical supplies.   Elektrobedarfsartikel.
ay-LEK-troh-buh-dahrfs-ahr-tee-kuhl.

1671. Employment agency.
Stellenvermittlungsbüro (OR: Arbeitsnachweisstelle).
SHTEH-luhn-fer-mit-loongs-bēw-roh (OR: *AHR-būts-naahkh-vīs-shteh-luh*).

1672. Fish store.   Fischhandlung.
FISH-hahnt-loong.

1673. Florist.   Blumengeschäft.
BLOO-muhn-guh-sheft.

1674. Fruit store.   Obstgeschäft.
OHPST-guh-sheft.

1675. Funeral parlor.   Beerdigungsinstitut.
buh-AYR-dih-goongs-in-stee-tōot.

1676. Furniture store.   Möbelgeschäft.
MŪR-buhl-guh-sheft.

1677. Gift store.   Geschenkartikelladen.
guh-SHENGK-ahr-tee-kuhl-laah-duhn.

1678. Grocery store.   Lebensmittelgeschäft.
LAY-buhns-mih-tuhl-guh-sheft.

1679. Ladies' hairdresser.   Damenfriseur.
DAAH-muhn-free-zūrr.

1680. Hardware store.   Eisenwarengeschäft.
Ī-zuhn-vaah-ruhn-guh-sheft.

1681. Hat shop.   Hutladen.   *HŌŌT-laah-duhn.*

1682. Health food store.   Reformhaus.
reh-FAWRM-hows.

1683. Housewares.   Haushaltsartikel.
HOWS-hahlts-ahr-tee-kuhl.

1684. Jewelry store.   Juweliergeschäft.
yōō-vay-LEER-guh-sheft.

1685. Lawyer.   Rechtsanwalt (OR: Anwalt).
REKHTS-ahn-vahlt (OR: AHN-vahlt).

1686. Laundry.   Wäscherei.   *veh-shuh-RĪ.*

1687. Loans.   Darlehen.   *DAAHR-lay-uhn.*

1688. Lumberyard.   Holzplatz.   *HAWLTS-plahts.*

1689. Market.   Markt.   *mahrkt.*

1690. Money exchange.   Wechselstube.
VEK-suhl-shtōō-buh.

1691. Music store.   Musikgeschäft.
mōō-ZEEK-guh-sheft.

1692. Musical instruments.   Musikinstrumente.
mōō-ZEEK-in-strōō-men-tuh.

1693. Newsstand.   Zeitungskiosk.
TSĪ-toongs-kee-awsk.

1694. Paints.   Farben.   *FAHR-buhn.*

1695. Pastry shop.   Konditorei.   *kawn-dee-toh-RĪ.*

1696. Pet shop.   Tierhandlung.
TEER-hahnt-loong.

1697. Photographer.
Photograph (OR: Fotograf) (F.: Photographin
  [OR: Fotografin]).
foh-toh-GRAAHF (F.: foh-toh-GRAAH-fin).

1698. Printing. Druckerei. *droo-kuh-RĪ.*

1699. Real estate.
Immobiliengesellschaft (OR: Immobilien).
ih-moh-BEE-lee-uhn-guh-zel-shahft (OR: *ih-mo-BEE-lee-uhn).*

1700. Sewing machines. Nähmaschinen.
NAY-mah-shee-nuhn.

1701. Shoemaker. Schuhmacher (OR: Schuster).
SHŌŌ-mah-khuhr (OR: *SHŌŌS-tuhr).*

1702. Shoe store. Schuhgeschäft.
SHŌŌ-guh-sheft.

1703. Sign painter. Schildermaler.
SHIL-duhr-maah-luhr.

1704. Sporting goods store. Sportgeschäft.
SHPAWRT-guh-sheft.

1705. Stockbroker. Börsenmakler.
BUR-zuhn-maahk-luhr.

1706. Supermarket. Supermarkt.
ZOO-puhr-mahrkt.

1707. Tailor. Schneider. *SHNĪ-duhr.*

1708. Toy shop. Spielwarengeschäft.
SHPEEL-vaah-ruhn-guh-sheft.

1709. Trucking. Fuhrunternehmen.
FŌŌR-oon-tuhr-nay-muhn.

1710. Upholsterer. Polsterer. *PAWL-stuh-ruhr.*

1711. Used cars. Gebrauchte Wagen.
guh-BROWKH-tuh VAAH-guhn.

1712. Vegetable store. Gemüseladen.
guh-MEW-zuh-laah-duhn.

1713. Watchmaker.   Uhrmacher.
ŌŌR-mah-khuhr.

1714. Wines and liquors.   Spirituosenhandlung.
shpee-ree-tŌŌ-OH-zuhn-hahnt-loong.

BABY CARE

1715. I need a reliable babysitter tonight [at 7 o'clock].
Ich brauche einen zuverlässigen Babysitter [um sieben
   Uhr] heute abend.
*ikh BROW-khuh Ī-nuhn TSŌŌ-fer-leh-sih-guhn
   "babysitter" [oom ZEE-buhn ōōr] HOY-tuh AAH-
   buhnt.*

1716. Call a pediatrician immediately.
Rufen Sie sofort einen Kinderarzt an!
*RŌŌ-fuhn zee zoh-FAWRT Ī-nuhn KIN-duhr-aahrtst
   ahn!*

1717. Change the diaper (LIT.: Lay the baby dry).
Legen Sie das Baby trocken!
LAY-guhn zee dahs "baby" TRAW-kuhn!

1718. Bathe the baby.
Baden Sie das Baby (OR: Kind)!
BAAH-duhn zee dahs "baby" (OR: kint)!

1719. Put the baby in the crib for a nap.
Legen Sie das Baby ins Kinderbett, damit es ein
   Schläfchen machen kann!
*LAY-guhn zee dahs "baby" ins KIN-duhr-bet, dah-MIT
   es īn SHLAYF-khuhn MAH-khuhn kahn!*

1720. Give the baby a pacifier if he (OR: she) **cries.**
Wenn das Baby weint, geben Sie ihm einen Schnuller!
*ven dahs "baby" vīnt, GAY-buhn zee eem Ī-nuhn
   SHNŌŌ-luhr!*

1721. Do you have an oitment for diaper rash?
Haben Sie eine Salbe gegen Wundsein?
HAAH-buhn zee Ī-nuh ZAHL-buh GAY-guhn
VOONT-zīn?

1722. Take the baby to the park in the [carriage] [stroller].
Bringen Sie das Baby zum Park in dem [Kinderwagen] [Sportwagen]!
BRING-uhn zee dahs "baby" tsoom pahrk in daym
[KIN-duhr-vaah-guhn] [SHPAWRT-vaah-guhn]!

1723. Baby (OR: **strained) food.**
Babynahrung. *"BABY"-naah-roong.*

1724. Baby powder. Babypuder.
"BABY"-pōō-duhr.

1725. Bib. Lätzchen. *LETS-k̄huhn.*

1726. Colic. Kolik. *KOH-lik.*

1727. Disposable bottles. Wegwerfflaschen.
VEK-verf-flah-shuhn.

1728. Disposable diapers. Papierwindeln.
pah-PEER-vin-duhln.

1729. High chair. Kinderstuhl. *KIN-duhr-shtōōl.*

1730. Nursemaid. Kindermädchen.
KIN-duhr-mayt-k̄huhn.

1731. Playground. Spielplatz. *SHPEEL-plahts.*

1732. Rattle. Klapper (OR: **Kinderklapper).**
KLAH-puhr (OR: *KIN-duhr-klah-puhr).*

1733. Stuffed animal. Stofftier. *SHTAWF-teer.*

HEALTH AND ILLNESS

1734. Is the doctor in the office?
Ist der Herr Doktor (F.: die Frau Doktor) im
  Sprechzimmer?
*ist dayr her DAWK-tawr (F.: dee frow DAWK-tawr) im
  SHPREKH-tsih-muhr?*

1735. What (LIT.: When) are [his] [her] office hours?
Wann sind [seine] [ihre] Sprechstunden?
vahn zint [ZĪ-nuh] [EE-ruh] SHPREKH-shtoon-duhn?

1736. Take [my temperature] [my blood pressure].
Messen Sie [meine Temperatur] [meinen Blutdruck]!
*MEH-suhn zee [MĪ-nuh tem-puh-rah-TOOR] [MĪ-nuhn
  BLOOT-drook]!*

1737. I have something in my eye.
Mir ist etwas ins Auge geflogen.
meer ist ET-vahs ins OW-guh guh-FLOH-guhn.

1738. I have a pain [in my back].
Ich habe Schmerzen [im Rücken].
ikh HAAH-buh SHMER-tsuhn [im REW-kuhn].

1739. [My toe] is swollen.
[Mein Zeh (OR: Meine Zehe)] ist geschwollen.
*[mīn tsay (OR: MĪ-nuh TSAY-uh)] ist guh-SHVAW-
  luhn.*

1740. It's sensitive to pressure.
Es ist empfindlich gegen Druck.
es ist emp-FINT-likh GAY-guhn drook.

1741. Is it serious?   Ist es ernst?
ist es ernst?

1742. I don't sleep well.   Ich schlafe nicht gut.
ikh SHLAAH-fuh nikht gōōt.

1743. I have no appetite.   Ich habe keinen Appetit.
ikh HAAH-buh KĪ-nuhn ah-pay-TEET.

1744. Can you give me something to relieve the pain?
Können Sie mir etwas gegen die Schmerzen geben?
*KUR-nuhn zee meer ET-vahs GAY-guhn dee SHMER-
tsuhn GAY-buhn?*

1745. I'm allergic to [penicillin].
Ich bin allergisch gegen [Penicillin].
ikh bin ah-LER-gish GAY-guhn [pay-nee-tsih-LEEN].

1746. Where should I have this prescription filled?
Wo soll ich dieses Rezept anfertigen (OR: zubereiten)
lassen?
*voh zawl ikh DEE-zuhs ray-TSEPT AHN-fer-tih-guhn
(OR: TSOO-buh-rī-tuhn) LAH-suhn?*

1747. Do I have to go to a hospital?
Muß ich in ein Krankenhaus (OR: Spital) gehen?
*moos ikh in īn KRAHNG-kuhn-hows (OR: shpee-
TAAHL) GAY-uhn?*

1748. Is surgery (LIT.: an operation) required?
Ist eine Operation nötig?
ist Ī-nuh oh-puh-rah-tsee-OHN NUR-tikh?

1749. Do I have to stay in bed?
Muß ich im Bett bleiben?
moos ikh im bet BLĪ-buhn?

1750. When will I begin to feel better?
Wann werde ich mich besser fühlen?
vahn VAYR-duh ikh mikh BEH-suhr FEW-luhn?

1751. Is it contagious?   Ist es ansteckend?
ist es AHN-shteh-kuhnt?

1752. I feel [better].   Ich fühle mich [besser].
ikh FEW-luh mikh [BEH-suhr].

1753. —worse. —schlechter. —*SHLEKH-tuhr.*

1754. —about the same as earlier.
—ungefähr genauso wie vorher.
—*OON-guh-fayr guh-NOW-zoh vee FOHR-hayr.*

1755. Shall I keep it bandaged?
Soll ich es verbunden halten?
zawl ikh es fer-BOON-duhn HAHL-tuhn?

1756. Can I travel [on Monday]?
Kann ich [(am) Montag] reisen?
kahn ikh [(ahm) MOHN-taahk] RĪ-zuhn?

1757. When will you come again?
Wann werden Sie wieder kommen?
vahn VAYR-duhn zee VEE-duhr KAW-muhn?

1758. When should I take [the medicine] [the pills]?
Wann soll ich [die Arznei (OR: das Medikament)] [die
Pillen] einnehmen?
*vahn zawl ikh [dee aahrts-NĪ (OR: dahs may-dee-kah-
MENT)] [dee PIH-luhn] ĪN-nay-muhn?*

**1759. When should I [give myself] [be given] the
injections?**
Wann soll ich mir die Injektionen (OR: Einspritzungen)
[geben] [geben lassen]?
*vahn zawl ikh meer dee in-yek-tsee-OH-nuhn (OR: ĪN-
shprih-tsoong-uhn) [GAY-buhn] [GAY-buhn LAH-
suhn]?*

1760. Every hour. Jede Stunde.
YAY-duh SHTOON-duh.

1761. [Before] [After] meals.
[Vor] [Nach] den Mahlzeiten.
[fohr] [naahkh] dayn MAAHL-tsī-tuhn.

1762. On an empty stomach.
Auf nüchternen Magen.
owf NEWKH-tuhr-nuhn MAAH-guhn.

1763. On going to bed.   Vor dem Schlafengehen.
fohr daym SHLAAH-fuhn-gay-uhn.

1764. On getting up.   Beim Aufstehen.
bīm OWF-shtay-uhn.

1765. Twice a day.   Zweimal täglich.
TSVĪ-maahl TAYK-likh.

1766. Anesthetic.   Betäubungsmittel.
buh-TOY-boongs-mih-tuhl.

1767. Convalescence.   Genesung.   *guh-NAY-zoong.*

1768. Cure.   Kur (OR: Heilverfahren).
kōōr (OR: HĪL-fer-faah-ruhn).

1769. Diet.   Diät.   *dee-AYT.*

1770. (A) drop.   Tropfen.   *TRAWP-fuhn.*

1771. Nurse.   Krankenpfleger (F.: Krankenpflegerin
OR Krankenschwester).
KRAHNG-kuhn-pflay-guhr (F.: KRAHNG-kuhn-pflay-guh-rin OR KRAHNG-kuhn-shves-tuhr).

1772. Ophthalmologist.   Augenarzt (F.: Augenärztin).
OW-guhn-aahrtst (F.: OW-guhn-erts-tin).

1773. Orthopedist.   Orthopäde.   *awr-toh-PAY-duh.*

1774. Remedy.   Hilfsmittel.   *HILFS-mih-tuhl.*

1775. Specialist.   Facharzt (F.: Fachärztin).
FAHKH-aahrtst (F.: FAHKH-erts-tin).

1776. Surgeon.   Chirurg.   *khee-ROORK.*

1777. Treatment.   Behandlung.
buh-HAHNT-loong.

1778. X rays. Röntgenstrahlen.
RURNT-guhn-shtraah-luhn.

AILMENTS

1779. Abscess. Abszeß. *ahps-TSES.*

1780. Allergy. Allergie. *ah-ler-GEE.*

1781. Appendicitis attack. Blinddarmentzündung.
BLINT-dahrm-ent-tsewn-doong.

1782. Insect bite. Insektenstich.
in-ZEK-tuhn-shtik͟h.

1783. Blister. Blase. *BLAAH-zuh.*

1784. Boil. Furunkel. *fo͞o-ROONG-kuhl.*

1785. Bruise. Quetschung. *KVET-shoong.*

1786. Burn. Verbrennung (OR: Brandwunde).
fer-BREH-noong (OR: BRAHNT-voon-duh).

1787. Chicken. Windpocken. *VINT-paw-kuhn.*

1788. Chill. Schüttelfrost. *SHEW-tuhl-frawst.*

1789. Cold. Erkältung.* *er-KEL-toong.*

1790. Constipation. Verstopfung.
fer-SHTAWP-foong.

1791. Corn. Hühnerauge. *HĒW-nuhr-ow-guh.*

1792. Cough. Husten. *HO͞OS-tuhn.*

1793. Cramp. Krampf. *krahmpf.*

1794. Cut. Schnittwunde. *SHNIT-voon-duh.*

1795. Diarrhea. Durchfall. *DOORK͟H-fahl.*

1796. Dysentery. Ruhr. *ro͞or.*

*In Austria: Verkühlung (*fer-KĒW-loong*).

1797. Earache. Ohrenschmerzen.
OH-ruhn-shmer-tsuhn.

1798. To feel faint. Sich der Ohnmacht nahe fühlen.
zikh dayr OHN-makht NAAH-uh FEW-luhn.

1799. Fever. Fieber. *FEE-buhr.*

1800. Fracture. Bruch. *brookh.*

1801. Hay fever. Heuschnupfen.
HOY-shnoop-fuhn.

1802. Headache. Kopfschmerzen.
KAWPF-shmer-tsuhn.

1803. Indigestion. Verdauungsstörung (OR:
Magenverstimmung).
fer-DOW-oongs-shtūr-roong (OR: MAAH-guhn-fer-shtih-moong).

1804. Infection. Infektion. *in-fek-tsee-OHN.*

1805. Inflammation. Entzündung.
ent-TSEWN-doong.

1806. Influenza (OR: Flu). Grippe. *GRIH-puh.*

1807. Insomnia. Schlaflosigkeit.
SHLAAHF-loh-zikh-kīt.

1808. Measles. Masern. *MAAH-zuhrn.*

1809. German measles (OR: Rubella).
Röteln. *RŪR-tuhln.*

1810. Mumps. Ziegenpeter (OR: Mumps).
TSEE-guhn-pay-tuhr (OR: moomps).

1811. Nausea. Übelkeit. *EW-buhl-kīt.*

1812. Nosebleed. Nasenbluten.
NAAH-zuhn-bloo-tuhn.

1813. Pneumonia. Lungenentzündung.
LOONG-uhn-ent-tsewn-doong.

1814. Poisoning. Vergiftung. *fer-GIF-toong.*

1815. Sinusitis. Stirnhöhlenentzündung.
SHTIRN-hūr-luhn-ent-tsewn-doong.

1816. A sore throat. Halsschmerzen.
HAHLS-shmer-tsuhn.

1817. Sprain. Verstauchung (OR: Verrenkung).
fer-SHTOW-khoong (OR: fer-RENG-koong).

1818. Bee sting. Bienenstich. *BEE-nuhn-shtĩkh.*

1819. Sunburn. Sonnenbrand. *ZAW-nuhn-brahnt.*

1820. Swelling (OR: growth).
Schwellung (OR: Geschwulst).
SHVEH-loong (OR: guh-SHVOOLST).

1821. Tonsillitis. Mandelentzündung.
MAHN-duhl-ent-tsewn-doong.

1822. To vomit. Erbrechen (OR: Sich übergeben).
er-BREH-khuhn (OR: zĩkh ēw-buhr-GAY-buhn).

See also "Accidents," "Parts of the Body" and
"Pharmacy."

DENTIST

1823. Can you recommend [a good dentist]?
Können Sie [einen guten Zahnarzt] empfehlen?
KUR-nuhn zee [Ī-nuhn GOO-tuhn TSAAHN-aahrtst]
emp-FAY-luhn?

1824. I've lost a filling.
Ich habe eine Plombe (OR: Füllung) verloren.
*ikh HAAH-buh Ī-nuh PLAWM-buh (OR: FEW-loong)
fer-LOH-ruhn.*

1825. Can you replace [the filling]?
Können Sie [die Plombe] ersetzen?
KUR-nuhn zee [dee PLAWM-buh] er-ZEH-tsuhn?

1826. Can you fix [the bridge] [this denture]?
Können Sie [die Brücke] [diese Prothese] reparieren?
*KUR-nuhn zee [dee BREW-kuh] [DEE-zuh proh-TAY-
zuh] ray-pah-REE-ruhn?*

1827. [This tooth] hurts.   [Dieser Zahn] schmerzt.
[DEE-zuhr tsaahn] shmertst.

1828. My gums are sore.   Das Zahnfleisch ist wund.
dahs TSAAHN-flish ist voont.

1829. I have [a broken tooth].
Ich habe [einen gebrochenen Zahn].
*ikh HAAH-buh [Ī-nuhn guh-BRAW-khuh-nuhn
tsaahn].*

1830. —a toothache.   —Zahnschmerzen.
—TSAAHN-shmer-tsuhn.

1831. —a cavity.   —ein Loch.   *—īn lawkh.*

**1832. Give me [a general anesthetic] [a local
anesthetic].**
Geben Sie mir [eine Vollnarkose] [ein örtliches
Betäubungsmittel]!
*GAY-buhn zee meer [Ī-nuh FAWL-nahr-koh-zuh] [īn
URRT-lih-khuhs buh-TOY-boongs-mih-tuhl]!*

1833. I [don't] want the tooth extracted.
Ich möchte den Zahn [nicht] ziehen lassen.
*ikh MURKH-tuh dayn tsaahn [nikht] TSEE-uhn LAH-
suhn.*

1834. A temporary filling. Eine provisorische Plombe.

Ī-nuh proh-vee-ZOH-rih-shuh PLAWM-buh.

ACCIDENTS

1835. There's been an accident.
Es ist ein Unfall passiert.
es ist īn OON-fahl pah-SEERT.

1836. Call [a doctor] immediately.
Rufen Sie sofort [einen Arzt]!
RŌŌ-fuhn zee zoh-FAWRT [Ī-nuhn aahrtst]!

1837. —an ambulance. —einen Krankenwagen.
—Ī-nuhn KRAHNG-kuhn-vaah-guhn.

1838. —a police officer.
—einen Polizisten (F.: eine Polizistin).
—Ī-nuhn poh-lee-TSIS-tuhn (F.: Ī-nuh poh-lee-TSIS-tin).

1839. [He] [She] has fallen. [Er] [Sie] ist gefallen.
[er] [zee] ist guh-FAH-luhn.

1840. [He] [She] has fainted.
[Er] [Sie] ist in Ohnmacht gefallen.
[er] [zee] ist in OHN-mahkht guh-FAH-luhn.

1841. Don't move [him] [her].
Bewegen Sie [ihn] [sie] nicht!
buh-VAY-guhn zee [een] [zee] nikht!

1842. [My finger] is bleeding. [Der Finger] blutet.
[dayr FING-uhr] BLŌŌ-tuht.

1843. A fracture. Ein Bruch. *īn brookh.*

1844. A fracture of the arm. Ein Armbruch.
īn AHRM-brookh.

1845. A fracture of the leg.   Ein Beinbruch.
īn BĪN-brookh.

1846. I want [to rest].   Ich möchte mich [ausruhen].
ikh MURKH-tuh mikh [OWS-rōō-uhn].

1847. —to sit down.   —hinsetzen.
—HIN-zeh-tsuhn.

1848. —to lie down.   —hinlegen.   *—HIN-lay-guhn.*

1849. Notify [my husband] [my wife].
Benachrichtigen Sie [meinen Mann] [meine Frau]!
buh-NAAHKH-rikh-tih-guhn zee [MĪ-nuhn mahn] [MĪ-nuh frow]!

1850. A tourniquet.   Eine Aderpresse.
Ī-nuh AAH-duhr-preh-suh.

PARTS OF THE BODY

1851. Ankle.   Knöchel.   *KNUR-khuhl.*

1852. Appendix.   Blinddarm.   *BLINT-dahrm.*

1853. Arm.   Arm.   *ahrm.*

1854. Armpit.   Achselhöhle.   *AHK-suhl-hūr-luh.*

1855. Artery.   Schlagader (OR: Pulsader).
SHLAAHK-aah-duhr (OR: POOLS-aah-duhr).

1856. Back.   Rücken.   *REW-kuhn.*

1857. Belly.   Bauch.   *bowkh.*

1858. Bladder.   Blase.   *BLAAH-zuh.*

1859. Blood.   Blut.   *blōōt.*

1860. Blood vessel.   Blutgefäß.   *BLŌŌT-guh-fays.*

1861. Body.   Körper.   *KURR-puhr.*

1862. Bone.   Knochen.   *KNAW-khuhn.*

1863. Bowel. Darm. *dahrm.*

1864. Brain. Gehirn. *guh-HIRN.*

1865. Breast. Brust. *broost.*

1866. Calf. Wade. *VAAH-duh.*

1867. Cheek. Backe. *BAH-kuh.*

1868. Chest. Brustkorb. *BROOST-kawrp.*

1869. Chin. Kinn. *kin.*

1870. Collarbone. Schlüsselbein.
SHLEW-suhl-bīn.

1871. Ear. Ohr. *ohr.*

1872. Elbow. Ellbogen. *EL-boh-guhn.*

1873. Eye. Auge. *OW-guh.*

1874. Eyelashes. Augenwimpern.
OW-guhn-vim-puhrn.

1875. Eyelid. Augenlid. *OW-guhn-leet.*

1876. Face. Gesicht. *guh-ZĪKHT.*

1877. Finger. Finger. *FING-uhr.*

1878. Fingernail. Fingernagel.
FING-uhr-naah-guhl.

1879. Foot. Fuß. *foos.*

1880. Forehead. Stirne. *SHTIR-nuh.*

1881. Gall bladder. Gallenblase.
GAH-luhn-blaah-zuh.

1882. Genitals. Geschlechtsteile.
guh-SHLEKHTS-tī-luh.

1883. Glands. Drüsen. *DREW-zuhn.*

1884. Gums. Zahnfleisch. *TSAAHN-flīsh.*

1885. Hair. Haare (OR: Haar).
HAAH-ruh (OR: *haahr*).

1886. Hand. Hand. *hahnt.*

1887. Head. Kopf. *kawpf.*

1888. Heart. Herz. *herts.*

1889. Heel. Ferse. *FER-zuh.*

1890. Hip. Hüfte. *HEWF-tuh.*

1891. Intestines. Darm (OR: Eingeweide).
dahrm (OR: *ĪN-guh-vī-duh*).

1892. Jaw. Kiefer. *KEE-fuhr.*

1893. Joint. Gelenk. *guh-LENK.*

1894. Kidney. Niere. *NEE-ruh.*

1895. Knee. Knie. *knee.*

1896. Larynx. Kehlkopf. *KAYL-kawpf.*

1897. Leg. Bein. *bīn.*

1898. Lip. Lippe. *LIH-puh.*

1899. Liver. Leber. *LAY-buhr.*

1900. Lungs. Lungen. *LOONG-uhn.*

1901. Mouth. Mund. *moont.*

1902. Muscle. Muskel. *MOOS-kuhl.*

1903. Navel. Nabel. *NAAH-buhl.*

1904. Neck. Hals. *hahls.*

1905. Nerve. Nerv. *nerf.*

1906. Nose. Nase. *NAAH-zuh.*

1907. Pancreas. Bauchspeicheldrüse.
BOWKH-shpī-khuhl-drew-zuh.

1908. Rib. Rippe. *RIH-puh.*

1909. Shoulder. Schulter. *SHOOL-tuhr.*

1910. Side. Seite. *ZĪ-tuh.*

1911. Skin. Haut. *howt.*

1912. Skull. Schädel. *SHAY-duhl.*

1913. Spine. Wirbelsäule. *VIR-buhl-zoy-luh.*

1914. Spleen. Milz. *milts.*

1915. Stomach. Magen. *MAAH-guhn.*

1916. Temple. Schläfe. *SHLAY-fuh.*

1917. Thigh. Schenkel. *SHENG-kuhl.*

1918. Throat. Hals. *hahls.*

1919. Thumb. Daumen. *DOW-muhn.*

1920. Toe. Zeh (OR: Zehe). *tsay* (OR: *TSAY-uh*).

1921. Tongue. Zunge. *TSOONG-uh.*

1922. Tonsils. Mandeln. *MAHN-duhln.*

1923. Vein. Vene (OR: Ader).
VAY-nuh (OR: *AAH-duhr*).

1924. Waist. Taille. *TAHL-yuh.*

1925. Wrist. Handgelenk. *HAHNT-guh-lengk.*

TIME

1926. What time is it?
Wie spät ist es? (OR: Wieviel Uhr ist es?)
vee shpayt ist es? (OR: *VEE-feel ōōr ist es?*)

1927. Two [A.M.] [P.M.] (LIT.:[at night] [in the afternoon).
Zwei Uhr [nachts] [nachmittags].
tsvī ōōr [nahkhts] [NAAHKH-mih-taahks].

1928. Seven [A.M.] [P.M.] (LIT.: [in the morning] [in the evening]).
Sieben Uhr [morgens (OR: früh)] [abends].
ZEE-buhn ōor [MAWR-guhns (OR: frew)] [AAH-buhnts].

1929. It's exactly [half-past three (LIT.: half of four)].
Es ist genau [halb vier].
es ist guh-NOW [hahlp feer].

1930. —a quarter past four (LIT.: a quarter of five).
—viertel fünf.*   —*FEER-tuhl fewnf.*

1931. —a quarter to five (LIT.: three quarters of five).
—dreiviertel fünf.†   —*DRĪ-feer-tuhl fewnf.*

1932. At ten minutes to six.
Um zehn Minuten vor sechs.
oom tsayn mee-NŌŌ-tuhn fohr zeks.

1933. At twenty minutes past seven.
Um zwanzig Minuten nach sieben.
oom TSVAHN-tsikh mee-NŌŌ-tuhn naahkh ZEE-buhn.

1934. It's [early] [late].   Es ist [früh] [spät].
es ist [frew] [shpayt].

1935. In the morning.   Morgens (OR: Am Morgen).
MAWR-guhns (OR: ahm MAWR-guhn).

1936. In the afternoon.
Nachmittags (OR: Am Nachmittag).
NAAHKH-mih-taahks (OR: ahm NAAHKH-mih-tahk).

---

*In northern and central Germany.: viertel nach vier (*FEER-tuhl naahkh feer*). In Switzerland: viertel ab vier (*FEER-tuhl ahp feer*).

†In northern Germany and Switzerland: viertel vor fünf (*FEER-tuhl fohr fewnf*).

1937. Tomorrow.   Morgen.   *MAWR-guhn.*

1938. In the evening.   Abends (OR: Am Abend).
AAH-buhnts (OR: *ahm AAH-buhnt*).

1939. At noon.   Mittags.   *MIH-taahks.*

1940. At midnight.   Mitternachts.
MIH-tuhr-nahkhts.

1941. During the day.   Tagsüber.
TAAHKS-ew̄-buhr.

1942. Every evening.   Jeden Abend.
YAY-duhn AAH-buhnt.

1943. All night.   Die ganze Nacht hindurch.
dee GAHN-tsuh nahkht hin-DOORKH.

1944. Since yesterday.   Seit gestern.
zīt GES-tuhrn.

1945. Today.   Heute.   *HOY-tuh.*

1946. Tonight (OR: **This evening**).   Heute abend.
HOY-tuh AAH-buhnt.

1947. Last month.   Vorigen (OR: Letzten) Monat.
FOH-rih-guhn (OR: *LETS-tuhn) MOH-naht.*

1948. Last year.   Voriges (OR: Letztes) Jahr.
FOH-rih-guhs (OR: *LETS-tuhs) yaahr.*

1949. Next Sunday.
Nächsten Sonntag (OR: Am kommenden Sonntag).
NAYKH-stuhn ZAWN-taahk (OR: *ahm KAW-muhn-
duhn ZAWN-taahk).*

1950. Next week.   Nächste Woche.
NAYKH-stuh VAW-khuh.

1951. The day before yesterday.   Vorgestern.
FOHR-ges-tuhrn.

1952. The day after tomorrow.　Übermorgen.
EW-buhr-mawr-guhn.

1953. Two weeks ago.　Vor zwei Wochen.
fohr tsvī VAW-khuhn.

WEATHER

1954. How's the weather today?
Wie ist das Wetter heute?
vee ist dahs VEH-tuhr HOY-tuh?

1955. It looks like rain.　Es sieht nach Regen aus.
es zeet naahkh RAY-guhn ows.

1956. It's [cold].　Es ist [kalt].　*es ist [kahlt].*

1957. —fair.　—schön.　*—shūrn.*

1958. —warm.　—warm.　*—vahrm.*

1959. —windy.　—windig.　*—VIN-dikh.*

1960. —foggy.　—nebelig.　*—NAY-buh-likh.*

1961. The weather is clearing.
Das Wetter klärt sich auf.
dahs VEH-tuhr klayrt zikh owf.

1962. The weather is bad.　Das Wetter ist schlecht.
dahs VEH-tuhr ist shlekht.

1963. What a beautiful day!
Was für ein herrlicher Tag!
vahs fewr īn HER-lih-khuhr taahk!

1964. I want to sit [in the shade] [in the sun].
Ich möchte [im Schatten] [in der Sonne] sitzen.
*ikh MURKH-tuh [im SHAH-tuhn] [in dayr ZAW-nuh]
ZIH-tsuhn.*

1965. I want to sit in a breeze (LIT.: Where a breeze is blowing).
Ich möchte sitzen, wo eine Brise weht.
ikh MURK̄H-tuh ZIH-tsuhn, voh Ī-nuh BREE-zuh vayt).

1966. What is the weather forecast [for tomorrow] [for the weekend]?
Was ist die Wettervorhersage [für morgen] [für das Wochenende]?
vahs ist dee VEH-tuhr-fohr-hayr-zaah-guh [fewr MAWR-guhn] [fewr dahs VAW-khuhn-en-duh]?

1967. It will snow tomorrow.   Morgen schneit es.
MAWR-guhn shnīt es.

DAYS OF THE WEEK

1968. Sunday.   Sonntag.   *ZAWN-taahk.*
1969. Monday.   Montag.   *MOHN-taahk.*
1970. Tuesday.   Dienstag.   *DEENS-taahk.*
1971. Wednesday.   Mittwoch.   *MIT-vawkh.*
1972. Thursday.   Donnerstag.   *DAW-nuhrs-taahk.*
1973. Friday.   Freitag.   *FRĪ-taahk.*
1974. Saturday.   Sonnabend.*   *ZAWN-aah-buhnt.*

HOLIDAYS

1975. Public holiday.   Öffentlicher Feiertag.
UR-fent-lih-k̄huhr FĪ-uhr-taahk.

*In central Germany, Austria and Switzerland: Samstag (*ZAHMS-taahk*).

1976. Religious holiday.   Religiöser Feiertag.
ray-lee-gee-ŪR-zuhr FĪ-uhr-taahk.

1977. Labor Day (on May 1).   Tag der Arbeit.
taahk dayr AHR-bĭt.

1978. Good Friday.   Karfreitag.   *kaahr-FRĪ-taahk.*

1979. Ascension.   Christi Himmelfahrt.
KRIS-tee HIH-muhl-faahrt.

1980. Whitmonday.   Pfingstmontag.
PFINGST-mohn-taahk.

1981. [Merry] Christmas.
[Fröhliche] Weihnachten (OR: [Frohes] Weih-
nachtsfest)!
*[FRŪR-lih-khuh] VĪ-nahkh-tuhn (OR: [FROH-uhs] VĪ-
nahkhts-fest)!*

1982. Happy Easter.
Fröhliche Ostern (OR: Frohes Osterfest)!
*FRŪR-lih-khuh OHS-tuhrn (OR: FROH-uhs OHS-tuhr-
fest)!*

1983. Happy New Year!   Glückliches Neujahr!
GLEWK-lih-khuhs NOY-yaahr!

1984. Happy birthday.
Herzliche Glückwünsche zum Geburtstag!
*HERTS-lih-khuh GLEWK-vewn-shuh tsoom guh-
BOORTS-taahk!*

1985. Happy anniversary.   Alles Gute zum Jubiläum!
AH-luhs GŌO-tuh tsoom yōo-bee-LAY-oom!

DATES, MONTHS AND SEASONS

1986. January.   Januar.*   *YAH-nōo-aahr.*

*In Austria: Jänner (*YEH-nuhr*).

1987. February. Februar.* *FAY-br$\overline{oo}$-aahr.*

1988. March. März. *merts.*

1989. April. April. *ah-PRIL.*

1990. May. Mai. *mī.*

1991. June. Juni. *Y$\overline{OO}$-nee.*

1992. July. Juli. *Y$\overline{OO}$-lee.*

1993. August. August. *ow-GOOST.*

1994. September. September. *zep-TEM-buhr.*

1995. October. Oktober. *awk-TOH-buhr.*

1996. November. November. *noh-VEM-buhr.*

1997. December. Dezember. *day-TSEM-buhr.*

1998. Spring. Frühling (OR: Frühjahr).
FREW-ling (OR: FREW-yaahr).

1999. Summer. Sommer. *ZAW-muhr.*

2000. Autumn (OR: Fall). Herbst. *herpst.*

2001. Winter. Winter. *VIN-tuhr.*

2002. Today is the 31st of May, 1987.
Heute ist der einunddreißigste Mai neunzehn-
hundertsiebenundachtzig.
*HOY-tuh ist dayr ĪN-oont-drī-sikh-stuh mī NOYN-
tsayn-hoon-duhrt-zee-buhn-oont-ahkh-tsikh.*

NUMBERS: CARDINALS

2003. Zero. Null. *nool.*

2004. One. Eins. *īns.*

*In Austria sometimes: Feber (*FAY-buhr*).

2005. Two.   Zwei (OR on phone: Zwo).
tsvī (OR: tsvoh).

2006. Three.   Drei.   *drī.*

2007. Four.   Vier.   *feer.*

2008. Five.   Fünf.   *fewnf.*

2009. Six.   Sechs.   *zeks.*

2010. Seven.   Sieben.   *ZEE-buhn.*

2011. Eight.   Acht.   *ahkht.*

2012. Nine.   Neun.   *noyn.*

2013. Ten.   Zehn.   *tsayn.*

2014. Eleven.   Elf.   *elf.*

2015. Twelve.   Zwölf.   *tsvurlf.*

2016. Thirteen.   Dreizehn.   *DRĪ-tsayn.*

2017. Fourteen.   Vierzehn.   *FEER-tsayn.*

2018. Fifteen.   Fünfzehn.   *FEWNF-tsayn.*

2019. Sixteen.   Sechzehn.   *ZEK̄H-tsayn.*

2020. Seventeen.   Siebzehn.   *ZEEP-tsayn.*

2021. Eighteen.   Achtzehn.   *AHKH-tsayn.*

2022. Nineteen.   Neunzehn.   *NOYN-tsayn.*

2023. Twenty.   Zwanzig.   *TSVAHN-tsik̄h.*

2024. Twenty-one.   Einundzwanzig.
ĪN-oont-tsvahn-tsik̄h.

2025. Twenty-five.   Fünfundzwanzig.
FEWNF-oont-tsvahn-tsik̄h.

2026. Thirty.   Dreißig.   *DRĪ-sik̄h.*

2027. Forty.   Vierzig.   *FEER-tsik̄h.*

2028. Fifty.   Fünfzig.   *FEWNF-tsik̄h.*

2029. Sixty.   Sechzig.   *ZEK̄H-tsik̄h.*

2030. Seventy.   Siebzig.   *ZEEP-tsĩkh.*

2031. Eighty.   Achtzig.   *AHKH-tsĩkh.*

2032. Ninety.   Neunzig.   *NOYN-tsĩkh.*

2033. One hundred.   Hundert (OR: Einhundert).
HOON-duhrt (OR: *ĨN-hoon-duhrt*).

2034. One hundred and one.
Hunderteins (OR: Einhunderteins).
HOON-duhrt-īns (OR: *ĨN-hoon-duhrt-īns*).

2035. One hundred and ten.   Einhundertzehn.
ĨN-hoon-duhrt-tsayn.

2036. Two hundred.   Zweihundert.
TSVĨ-hoon-duhrt.

2037. One thousand.   Tausend (OR: Eintausend).
TOW-zuhnt (OR: *ĨN-tow-zuhnt*).

2038. Three thousand.   Dreitausend.
DRĨ-tow-zuhnt.

2039. One hundred thousand.   Einhunderttausend.
ĨN-hoon-duhrt-tow-zuhnt.

2040. One million.   Eine Million.
Ĩ-nuh mih-lee-OHN.

NUMBERS: ORDINALS

2041. First.   Erste.*   *AYR-stuh.*

2042. Second.   Zweite.   *TSVĨ-tuh.*

2043. Third.   Dritte.   *DRIH-tuh.*

---

*In certain contexts ordinal numbers appear with endings other
than the *-e* ending given in this section. You should be understood, however, if you use the forms given here.

2044. Fourth. Vierte. *FEER-tuh.*

2045. Fifth. Fünfte. *FEWNF-tuh.*

2046. Sixth. Sechste. *ZEKS-tuh.*

2047. Seventh. Siebte. *ZEEP-tuh.*

2048. Eighth. Achte. *AHKH-tuh.*

2049. Ninth. Neunte. *NOYN-tuh.*

2050. Tenth. Zehnte. *TSAYN-tuh.*

2051. Twentieth. Zwanzigste.
TSVAHN-tsikh-stuh.

2052. Thirtieth. Dreißigste. *DRĪ-sikh-stuh.*

2053. Hundredth. Hundertste. *HOON-duhrt-stuh.*

2054. Thousandth. Tausendste. *TOW-zuhnt-stuh.*

2055. Millionth. Millionste. *mih-lee-OHN-stuh.*

QUANTITIES

2056. A fraction. Ein Bruch. *īn brookh.*

2057. One-quarter. Ein Viertel. *īn FEER-tuhl.*

2058. One-third. Ein Drittel. *īn DRIH-tuhl.*

2059. One-half. Eine Hälfte. *Ī-nuh HELF-tuh.*

2060. Three-quarters. Dreiviertel. *DRĪ-feer-tuhl.*

2061. The whole. Das Ganze. *dahs GAHN-tsuh.*

2062. A few. Einige (OR: Ein paar).
Ī-nih-guh (OR: *īn paahr*).

2063. Several. Mehrere. *MAY-ruh-ruh.*

2064. Many. Viele. *FEE-luh.*

FAMILY

2065. Wife. Frau. *frow.*

2066. Husband. Mann. *mahn.*

2067. Mother. Mutter. *MOO-tuhr.*

2068. Father. Vater. *FAAH-tuhr.*

2069. Grandmother. Großmutter. *GROHS-moo-tuhr.*

2070. Grandfather. Großvater. *GROHS-faah-tuhr.*

2071. Daughter. Tochter. *TAWKH-tuhr.*

2072. Son. Sohn. *zohn.*

2073. Sister. Schwester. *SHVES-tuhr.*

2074. Brother. Bruder. *BROO-duhr.*

2075. Aunt. Tante. *TAHN-tuh.*

2076. Uncle. Onkel. *AWNG-kuhl.*

2077. Niece. Nichte. *NIKH-tuh.*

2078. Nephew. Neffe. *NEH-fuh.*

2079. Cousin. Vetter (F.: Kusine). *FEH-tuhr (F.: koo-ZEE-nuh).*

2080. Relatives. Verwandte. *fer-VAHNT-tuh.*

2081. Father-in-law. Schwiegervater. *SHVEE-guhr-faah-tuhr.*

2082. Mother-in-law. Schwiegermutter. *SHVEE-guhr-moo-tuhr.*

2083. Adults. Erwachsene. *er-VAHK-suh-nuh.*

2084. Children. Kinder. *KIN-duhr.*

COMMON SIGNS AND PUBLIC NOTICES

For ease of reference this section is alphabetized according to the German-language entries.

2085. Abfahrt. *AHP-faahrt.* Departure.

2086. Abfälle. *AHP-feh-luh.*
Refuse (OR: Garbage).

2087. Abort. *ahp-AWRT.* Toilet.

2088. Achtung. *AHKH-toong.* Attention.

2089. Amtliche Bekanntmachung.
AHMT-lih-k͞huh buh-KAHNT-mah-khoong.
Public notice.

2090. Ankleben verboten.
AHN-klay-buhn fer-BOH-tuhn. Post no bills.

2091. Ankunft. *AHN-koonft.* Arrival.

2092. Anschlagen verboten.
AHN-shlaah-guhn fer-BOH-tuhn. Post no bills.

2093. Aufzug. *OWF-ts͞ook.* Elevator.

2094. Ausgang. *OWS-gahng.* Exit.

2095. Auskunft. *OWS-koonft.* Information.

2096. Ausverkauf. *OWS-fer-kowf.*
Sale (OR: Clearance sale).

2097. Bahnhof (ABBREV.: **Bf.; Bhf.**). *BAAHN-hohf.*
Railroad station.

2098. Besetzt. *buh-ZETST.*
Engaged (OR: Occupied).

2099. Betreten des Rasens verboten.
buh-TRAY-tuhn des RAAH-zuhns fer-BOH-tuhn.
Keep off the grass.

2100. Betreten verboten.
buh-TRAY-tuhn fer-BOH-tuhn.   No trespassing.

2101. Betriebsferien.   *buh-TREEPS-fay-ree-uhn.*
Closed for vacation.

2102. Bibliothek.   *bee-blee-oh-TAYK.*   *Library.*

2103. Briefkasten.   *BREEF-kahs-tuhn.*   Mailbox.

2104. Bushaltestelle.
BOOS-hahl-tuh-shteh-luh.   Bus stop.

2105. Damen.   *DAAH-muhn.*
Ladies (OR: Ladies' room).

2106. Drücken.   *DREW-kuhn.*   Push.

2107. Eingang.   *ĪN-gahng.*   Entrance.

2108. Eintreten.   *ĪN-tray-tuhn.*   Enter.

2109. Eintritt.   *ĪN-trit.*   Admission.

2110. Eintritt frei.   *ĪN-trit frī.*   Admission free.

2111. Erfrischungen.
er-FRIH-shoong-uhn.   Refreshments.

2112. Fabrik.   *fah-BREEK.*   Factory.

2113. Fahrstuhl.   *FAAHR-shtool.*   Elevator.

2114. Fernsehen.   *FERN-zay-uhn.*   Television.

2115. Fernsprecher.
FERN-shpreh-khuhr.   Telephone.

2116. Frei.   *frī.*   Free (OR: Vacant).

2117. Friedhof.   *FREET-hohf.*   Cemetery.

2118. Frisch angestrichen (OR: **Frisch gestrichen**).
frish AHN-guh-shtrih-khuhn (OR: *frish guh-SHTRIH-khuhn*).
Fresh (OR: Wet) paint.

2119. [Nur] Fußgänger.
[nŌŌr] FŌŌS-geng-uhr. Pedestrians [only].

2120. Füttern der Tiere verboten.
FEW-tuhrn dayr TEE-ruh fer-BOH-tuhn.
Do not feed the animals.

2121. Gefahr. *guh-FAAHR.* Danger.

2122. Geöffnet 9–20.*
guh-URF-nuht noyn ŌŌr bis TSVAHN-tsikh ŌŌr.
Open from 9 A.M. to 8 P.M.

2123. Geschlossen 20–9.
guh-SHLAW-suhn TSVAHN-tsikh ŌŌr bis noyn ŌŌr.
Closed from 8 P.M. to 9 A.M.

2124. Geschlossen sonntags und feiertags.
guh-SHLAW-suhn ZAWN-taahks oont FĪ-uhr-taahks.
Closed on Sundays and holidays.

2125. Großhandel.
GROHS-hahn-duhl. Wholesale.

2126. Handelsschule. *HAHN-duhls-shŌŌ-luh.*
Business school.

2127. Haus zu vermieten. *hows tsŌŌ fer-MEE-tuhn.*
House for rent.

2128. Hausmeister. *HOWS-mīs-tuhr.* Janitor.

2129. Heiß. *hīs.* Hot.

2130. Herren. *HEH-ruhn.*
Gentlemen (OR: Men's room).

2131. Hier erhältlich. *heer er-HELT-likh.*
Sold here.

2132. Kalt. *kahlt.* Cold.

*Note that the 24-hour clock is used here.

2133. Kartenschalter. *KAHR-tuhn-shahl-tuhr.*
Ticket office (for train).

2134. Kasse. *KAH-suh.*
Ticket office (for theater, movies); cashier (for hotel, store).

2135. Kein Eingang [ausgenommen zu geschäftlichen Zwecken].
kīn IN-gahng [OWS-guh-naw-muhn tsoo guh-SHEFT-lih-khuhn TSVEH-kuhn].
No admittance [except on business].

2136. Keine Aufführung. *KĪ-nuh OWF-few-roong.*
No performance.

2137. Keine Vorstellung. *KĪ-nuh FOHR-shteh-loong.*
No performance.

2138. Kleinhandel. *KLĪN-hahn-duhl.* Retail.

2139. Kleinverkauf. *KLĪN-fer-kowf.* Retail.

2140. Klimageregelt. *KLEE-mah-guh-ray-guhlt.*
Air-conditioned.

2141. Klingeln. *KLING-uhln.* Ring the bell.

2142. Klinik. *KLEE-nik.* Clinic.

2143. Klosett. *kloh-ZET.* Toilet.

2144. Kostenlos. *KAWS-tuhn-lohs.* Free.

2145. Krankenhaus.
KRAHNG-kuhn-hows. Hospital.

2146. Läuten. (in Austria and Switzerland)
LOY-tuhn. Ring the bell.

2147. Lift. *lift.* Elevator.

2148. Links. *lingks.* To the left.

2149. Luftgekühlt. *LOOFT-guh-kēwlt.*
Air-conditioned.

2150. Männer.   *MEH-nuhr.*
Men (OR: Men's room).

2151. Mittagessen.   *MIH-taahk-eh-suhn.*   Lunch.

2152. Möblierte Zimmer frei (OR: zu vermieten).
*mūr-BLEER-tuh TSIH-muhr frī (OR: tsōō fer-MEE-
tuhn).*
Furnished rooms for rent.

2153. Müll.   *mewl.*   Refuse (OR: Garbage).

2154. Nach oben.   *naahkh OH-buhn.*   Up.

2155. Nach unten.   *naahkh OON-tuhn.*   Down.

2156. Notausgang.   *NOHT-ows-gahng.*
Emergency exit.

2157. Nur für Angestellte.
nōōr fewr AHN-guh-shtel-tuh.   Employees only.

2158. Offen.   *AW-fuhn.*   Open.

2159. Öffentlicher Fernsprecher.
UR-fuhnt-lih-k̄huhr FERN-shpreh-k̄huhr.
Public telephone.

2160. Pförtner.   *PFURT-nuhr.*   Janitor.

2161. Polizei.   *poh-lee-TSĪ.*   Police.

2162. Preisaktion.   *PRĪS-ahk-tsee-ohn.*   Bargain.

2163. Preisknuller.   *PRĪS-knoo-luhr.*   Bargain.

2164. Privatgrundstück.   *pree-VAHT-groont-shtewk.*
Private property.

2165. Privatweg.   *pree-VAHT-vayk.*   Private road.

2166. Rathaus.   *RAAHT-hows.*   City hall.

2167. Rauchen verboten.
ROW-khuhn fer-BOH-tuhn.   No smoking.

2168. Raucher.   *ROW-khuhr.*
Smoker (OR: Smoking car).

2169. Reserviert.   *ray-zer-VEERT.*   Reserved.

2170. Ruhe.   *ROO-uh.*   Quiet (OR: Silence).

2171. Schellen. (in central Germany)
SHEH-luhn.   Ring the bell.

2172. Schwimmen verboten.
SHVIH-muhn fer-BOH-tuhn.   No swimming.

2173. Selbstbedienung (OR: **S-B**).
ZELPST-buh-dee-noong (OR: *ES-BAY*).
Self-service.

2174. Speisesaal.   *SHPĪ-zuh-zaahl.*   Dining room.

2175. Speisewagen.   *SHPĪ-zuh-vaah-guhn.*
Dining car.

2176. Spital.   *shpee-TAAHL.*   Hospital.

2177. Spucken verboten.
SHPOO-kuhn fer-BOH-tuhn.   No spitting.

2178. Straßenarbeiten.
SHTRAAH-suhn-ahr-bī-tuhn.   Men at work.

2179. Taxenstand.   *TAH-ksuhn-shtahnt.*
Taxi stand.

2180. Tiergarten.   *TEER-gahr-tuhn.*   Zoo.

2181. Toilette.   *toh-ah-LEH-tuh.*   Toilet.

2182. Treppen.   *TREH-puhn.*   Stairs.

2183. Ununterbrochene Vorstellung.
OON-oon-tuhr-braw-khuh-nuh FOHR-shteh-loong.
Continuous performance.

2184. Verboten.   *fer-BOH-tuhn.*   Forbidden.

2185. Vorsicht Hund.   *FOHR-zikht hoont.*
Beware of dog.

2186. Vorsicht Stufe. *FOHR-zikht SHTOO-fuh.*
Watch your step.

2187. Warnung. *VAHR-noong.* Warning.

2188. Wartesaal. *VAHR-tuh-zaahl.* Waiting room.

2189. W.C. *vay-TSAY.* Toilet.

2190. Ziehen. *TSEE-uhn.* Pull.

2191. Zu vermieten. *tsoo fer-MEE-tuhn.* For rent.

2192. Zum Verkauf. *tscom fer-KOWF.* For sale.

2193. Zu den Zügen. *tsoo dayn TSEW-guhn.*
To the trains.

2194. Zurück [13 Uhr].
tsoo-REWK [DRĬ-tsayn oor].
Will return at [1 P.M.].

INDEX

The sentences, words and phrases in this book are numbered consecutively from 1 to 2194. The entries in the index refer to these numbers. In addition, each major section heading (capitalized entries) is indexed according to page number. In cases where the English entry is ambiguous, its part of speech is indicated by one of the following abbreviations: *adj.* for adjective, *adv.* for adverb, *n.* for noun, *prep.* for preposition and *v.* for verb. Parentheses are used for explanations, as they are in the body of the phrasebook.

Because of the large volume of material indexed, cross-indexing has generally been avoided. Phrases or groups of words will usually be found under only one of their components, e.g., "emergency exit" appears only under "emergency," even though there is a separate entry for "exit" alone. If you do not find a phrase under one word, try another.

Every English word or phrase in the index is followed by one or more German equivalents, which are ordinarily given in the standard dictionary form: the nominative singular for nouns, the uninflected form for adjectives and the infinitive for verbs. In order to provide additional information about the language, the index includes the gender or number of each German noun in parentheses: m. for masculine, f. for feminine, n. for neuter and pl. for plural.

In effect, the reader is provided with an up-to-date English-German glossary. Of course, a knowledge of German grammar is necessary for making the best use of this index, especially since German is an inflected language. To assist you in using the correct forms of words, the index lists all the sentences which contain different forms of a given word. For example, under "understand" (infinitive *verstehen*), sentences 119, 120 and 1439 are listed. They provide the forms *verstehe* (1st person singular), *verstehen* (2nd person polite) and *versteht* (3rd person singular), respectively. Invariable forms are indexed only once, and only one appearance of each different variation is listed, so that there are no duplicate listings. The beginner would do well to look at all the sentences listed for a German word in order to become familiar with the possible range of variations (and at all the German equivalents listed for an English word in order to become familiar with their different shades of meaning).

It is not the purpose of the present book to teach German grammar, but it will give you the proper form to look up in a dictionary, where you will find more information.

Where a numbered sentence contains a choice of German equivalents (e.g., entry 281, which gives both *Anmeldung* and *Meldung* for "announcement"), only the first choice has been included in the index. (Always refer to the numbered sentence for more information.)

Schnellverband (m.) 1451; — tape: *Heftpflaster* (n.) 1452

adjust: *nachstellen* 405; *regulieren* 1603

admission (charge): *Eintritt* (m.) 1164

admittance: *Eingang* (m.) 2135

adults: *Erwachsene* (pl.) 2083

advance, in: *im voraus* 1067

after: *nach* 1761

afternoon, in the: *nachmittags* 1936

again: *noch einmal* 551; *wieder* 1757

ago, two weeks: *vor zwei Wochen* 1953

ahead, straight: *geradeaus* 212

AILMENTS, p. 141

air: *Luft* (f.) 610; — filter: *Luftfilter* (m.) 415

air-conditioned: *klimageregelt* 2140; *luftgekühlt* 2149

air-conditioning: *Klimaanlage* (f.) 578

airline: *Fluglinie* (f.) 186

airmail: *Luftpost* (f.) 508;

— stationery: *Luftpostpapier* (n.) 1425

AIRPLANE, p. 23

airport: *Flughafen* (m.) 260

aisle: *Gang* (m.) 272

à la carte: *à la carte* 762

alarm clock: *Wecker* (m.) 681

alcohol: *Alkohol* (m.) 416

all (everything): *alles* 48; — right: *in Ordnung* 19

allergic: *allergisch* 1745

allergy: *Allergie* (f.) 1780

allowed, be: *dürfen* 37

allow me: *gestatten Sie* 15

alone (= in peace): *in Ruhe* 145

along: *entlang* 207

already: *schon* 515

also: *auch* 352

altar: *Altar* (m.) 1107

alteration: *Änderung* (f.) 1276

altogether: *alles zusammen* 1243; *insgesamt* 176

aluminum: *Aluminium* (n.) 1379

A.M. (= at night) *nachts* 1927; (= early) *früh* 1073; (= in the morning) *morgens* 1928

borrow: *borgen* 390
botanical: *botanisch* 1093
bother *(v.)*: *sich bemühen* 21
bottle: *Flasche* (f.) 720; disposable (baby) —: *Wegwerfflasche* (f.) 1727; — opener: *Flaschenöffner* (m.) 684
bottled: *in einer Flasche* 734
boulevard: *Boulevard* (m.) 207
bourbon whiskey: *Bourbon* (m.) 730
bowel: *Darm* (m.) 1863
box (theater): *Loge* (f.) 1132; —office: *Theaterkasse* (f.) 1145
boy: *Junge* (m.) 78
boyfriend: *Freund* (m.) 54
bracelet: *Armband* (n.) 1310
brain: *Gehirn* (n.) 1864
brains (food): *Gehirne* (pl.) 897
braised: *geschmort* 796
brake: *Bremse* (f.) 405; emergency —: *Notbremse* (f.) 420; foot —: *Fußbremse* (f.) 421; hand —: *Handbremse* (f.) 422;

— light: *Bremslicht* (n.) 466
brand: *Marke* (f.) 1236, 1570
brandy: *Weinbrand* (m.) 724
brass: *Messing* (n.) 1380
brassiere: *Büstenhalter* (m.) 1311
bread: *Brot* (n.) 772; dark —: *Schwarzbrot* (n.) 854; white —: *Weißbrot* (n.) 855
breaded: *paniert* 797
break (v.): *zerbrechen* 1281; — down (auto): *eine Panne haben* 386
breakfast: *Frühstück* (n.) 237
breast: *Brust* (f.) 1865
breeze: *Brise* (f.) 1965
bridge: *Brücke* (f.) 206, 1826; (cards): *Bridge* (n.) 1188
briefs: *kurze Unterhose* (f.) 1312
bring: *bringen* 620
broken: *gebrochen* 1829; *kaputt* 1595
broom: *Besen* (m.) 685
brother: *Bruder* (m.) 2074
brown: *braun* 1366

cauliflower: *Blumenkohl* (m.) 958; (Austria) *Karfiol* (m.) 972

cavity (dental): *Loch* (n.) 1831

celery: *Sellerie* (m., f.) 1007; — salad: *Selleriesalat* (m.) 889

cemetery: *Friedhof* (m.) 2117

ceramics: *Keramik* (f.) 1400

cereal: (cooked) *Brei* (m.) 860; (dry) *Getreideflocken* (pl.) 861

chair: *Stuhl* (m.) 687

CHAMBERMAID, p. 58

chambermaid: *Zimmermädchen* (n.) 621

champagne: *Sekt* (m.) 739

change: (*n.*, = the rest) *Rest* (m.) 345; small —: *Kleingeld* (n.) 1231; (*v.*) *wechseln* 391

charge: (*n.*) *Betrag* (m.) 828; minimum —: *Minimalgebühr* (f.) 528; what is the —: *was kostet* 1069; (*v.*) *berechnen* 333

chassis: *Fahrgestell* (n.) 425

cheaper: *billiger* 605

check: (*n.*, bill) *Rechnung* (f.) 823, 824; traveler's —: *Reisescheck* (m.) 1226; (*v.*) *prüfen* 398; (luggage) *aufgeben* 170; — in: *sich melden* 260; — out: *ausziehen* 644

checkers: *Dame* (f.) 1187

checkroom: *Garderobe* (f.) 1658

cheek: *Backe* (f.) 1867

cheese: *Käse* (m.) 1048

cherry: *Kirsche* (f.) 1028

chess: *Schach* (n.) 1186

chest (body): *Brustkorb* (m.) 1868

chest of drawers: *Kommode* (f.) 688

chewing gum: *Kaugummi* (m.) 1462

chicken: *Huhn* (n.) 924; breaded fried —: *Backhendl* (n.) 921; — salad: *Geflügelsalat* (m.) 873; — soup: *Hühnersuppe* (f.) 878

chicken pox: *Windpocken* (pl.) 1787

child: *Kind* (n.) 2084

chill (*n.*): *Schüttelfrost* (m.) 1788

chin: *Kinn* (n.) 1869

expressway: *Autobahn* 377

exterior (*n.*): *Außenseite* (f.) 435

external: *äußerlich* 1450

extract (*v.*): *ziehen* 1833

eye: *Auge* (n.) 1737; — cup: *Augenbecher* (m.) 1479; — wash: *Augenwasser* (n.) 1480

eyebrow: *Augenbraue* (f.) 1628

eyelash: *Augenwimper* (f.) 1874

eyelid: *Augenlid* (n.) 1875

face: *Gesicht* (n.) 1876; — powder: *Gesichtspuder* (m.) 1504

facial (*n.*): *Gesichtsmassage* (f.) 1641

factory: *Fabrik* (f.) 226

faint (*v.*): *in Ohnmacht fallen* 1840; feel —: *sich der Ohnmacht nahe fühlen* 1798

fair (weather): *schön* 1957

fall: (*n.*, season) *Herbst* (m.) 2000; (*v.*) *fallen* 1839

familiar; be — with: *kennen* 357

FAMILY, p. 159

fan (*n.*): *Ventilator* (m.) 436; — belt: *Ventilatorriemen* (m.) 437

far: *weit* 71

fare: *Fahrt* (f.) 320

fashionable: *modisch* 1251

fast, be (timepiece): *vorgehen* 1594

fasten: *binden* 1608

father: *Vater* (m.) 2068

father-in-law: *Schwiegervater* (m.) 2081

fatty: *fett* 784

faucet: *Wasserhahn* (m.) 655

fault: *Schuld* (f.) 142

February: *Februar* (m.) 1987

feed (animals): *füttern* 2120

feel: *sich fühlen* 1750, 1752

fender: *Kotflügel* (m.) 438

ferry: *Fähre* (f.) 243

fever: *Fieber* (n.) 1799

few, a: *einige* 174

fiction: *Prosaliteratur* (f.) 1415

fifteen: *fünfzehn* 2018

fifth: *fünfte* 2045

fifty: *fünfzig* 2028

fig: *Feige* (f.) 1026

fill (prescription): *an-*

folder: *Aktendeckel* (m.)
1416

folk dance: *Volkstanz*
(m.) 1176

follow: *folgen* 180

food: *Essen* (n.) 258

FOOD: SEASONINGS,
p. 72

foot: *Fuß* (m.) 1879; —
powder: *Fußpuder* (m.)
1505

footpath: *Fußpfad* (m.)
1211

for: *für* 52

forbidden: *verboten* 2184

forehead: *Stirne* (f.) 1880

foreign: *ausländisch* 1224

forest: *Wald* (m.) 1219

forget: *vergessen* 140

fork: (in road)
Abzweigung (f.) 378;
(utensil) *Gabel* (f.) 775

forty: *vierzig* 2027

forward (v.): *schicken* 521

four: *vier* 176

fourteen: *vierzehn* 2017

fourth: *vierte* 448, 2044

fox trot: *Foxtrott* (m.)
1171

fraction: *Bruch* (m.) 2056

fracture (n.): *Bruch* (m.)
1800; — of the arm:
Armbruch (m.) 1844;
— of the leg:
Beinbruch (m.) 1845

fragile: *zerbrechlich* 182,
514

free: (unoccupied) *frei*
332; (no charge) *frei*
2110; *kostenlos* 2144

French (n.): *Französisch*
115

fresh: *frisch* 785

Friday: *Freitag* (m.) 100;
Good —: *Karfreitag*
(m.) 1978

fried: *gebraten* 799

friend: (female) *Freundin*
54; (male) *Freund* 54

front: in — of: *vor* 219

frozen: *tiefgefroren* 786

fruit: — drink: *Fruchtsaft*
(m.) 734; — soup
(chilled): *kalte Obst-
suppe* (f.) 879; *Kalt-
schale* (f.) 880; — store:
Obstgeschäft (n.) 1674

FRUITS, p. 83

fuel pump: *Benzinpumpe*
(f.) 441

funeral parlor: *Beerdi-
gungsinstitut* (n.) 1675

fur: *Pelz* (m.) 1403

furnished: *möbliert* 673

furniture: *Möbel* (pl.) 611; piece of —: *Möbelstück* (n.) 1285; — store: *Möbelgeschäft* (n.) 1676

fuse: *Sicherung* (f.) 442

gall bladder: *Gallenblase* (f.) 1881

gallery, fine arts: *Kunstgalerie* (f.) 1102

gambling casino: *Spielkasino* (n.) 1148

game (meat): *Wild* (n.) 919

garage: *Garage* (f.) 381

garbage: *Abfälle* (pl.) 2086; *Müll* (m.) 2153; — receptacle: *Abfalleimer* (m.) 1212

garden: *Garten* (m.) 1093

garlic: *Knoblauch* (m.) 832

gas: (carbonation) *Kohlensäure* (f.) 720; (gasoline) *Benzin* (n.) 352; premium —: *Superbenzin* (n.) 395; regular —: *Normalbenzin* (n.) 394; — station: *Tankstelle* (f.) 383; — tank: *Benzintank* (m.) 443

gate, boarding: (plane) *Flugsteig* (m.) 276; (train) *Sperre* (f.) 304

gauze: *Verbandmull* (m.) 1482

gear: *Gang* (m.) 445; neutral —: *Leerlauf* (m.) 450; reverse —: *Rückwärtsgang* (m.) 449; — shift: *Schalthebel* (m.) 444

general delivery: *postlagernde Sendungen* (pl.) 523

generator: *Generator* (m.) 451

Geneva: *Genf* 170

genitals: *Geschlechtsteile* (pl.) 1882

gentlemen: *Herren* (pl.) 2130

German: (language) *Deutsch* 117; (nationality) *deutsch* 188

German measles: *Röteln* (pl.) 1809

get: (= obtain) *bekommen* 291; (= provide) *besorgen* 181; — off: *aussteigen* 294, 322; — there: *hinfahren* 338; *hinkommen* 135

getting up (awaking):
Aufstehen (n.) 1764
gift: *Geschenk* (n.) 166;
— store: *Geschenk-
artikelladen* (m.) 1677
GIFT AND SOUVENIR
LIST, p. 122
gin: *Gin* (m.) 726
girl: *Mädchen* (n.) 79
girlfriend: *Freundin* (f.)
54
give: *geben* 175
given, be: *(sich) geben
lassen* 1759
glad: *froh* 107
gland: *Drüse* (f.) 1883
glass: (n.) *Glas* (n.) 665
glasses (eye): *Brille* (f.)
1595
glove: *Handschuh* (m.)
1320; — compartment:
Handschuhfach (n.) 452
go: *gehen* 146, 186, 200;
fahren 319, 321; — out:
abgehen 517
gold: *Gold* (n.) 1382
golf: *Golf* (n.) 1182; —
equipment: *Golfaus-
rüstung* (f.) 1194
good: *gut* 2, 5, 562
goodbye: *auf Wiedersehen*
7; (on phone) *auf
Wiederhören* 546

goods: *Waren* (pl.) 168
goose: *Gans* (f.) 923
grandfather: *Großvater*
(m.) 2070
grandmother: *Großmutter*
(f.) 2069
grape: *Traube* (f.) 1038
grapefruit: *Pampelmuse*
(f.) 1033; — juice:
Pampelmusensaft (m.)
850
grass: *Rasen* (m.) 2099
gray: *grau* 1367
grease: *Schmierfett* (n.)
453
greasy: *fettig* 787
green: *grün* 1368;
olive —: *olivgrün* 1369
grilled: *gegrillt* 800
grocery store:
Lebensmittelgeschäft
(n.) 1678
guest (= visit): *Besuch*
(m.) 637
guide: *Führer* (m.) 1065
guidebook: *Reiseführer*
(m.) 1417
gums: *Zahnfleisch* (n.)
1828
gymnasium: *Turnhalle* (f.)
247

haddock: *Schellfisch* (m.)
949

ink: *Tinte* (f.) 1418
inn: *Gasthaus* (n.) 566
inner tube: *Schlauch* (m.) 460
insect bite: *Insektenstich* (m.) 1782
insecticide: *Insektenvertilgungsmittel* (n.) 656
inside: *in* 213
insomnia: *Schlaflosigkeit* (f.) 1807
instrument panel: *Armaturenbrett* (n.) 461
insurance: collision —: *Kaskoversicherung* (f.) 355; personal liability—: *Haftpflichtversicherung* (f.) 353; property damage —: *Sachschadenversicherung* (f.) 354
insure: *versichern* 516
interested: be — in: *sich interessieren für* 1078
interesting: *interessant* 1096
intermission: *Pause* (f.) 1140
internally: *innerlich* 1449
international: *international* 349
intersection: *Kreuzung* (f.) 379

intestines: *Darm* (m.) 1891
introduce: *bekanntmachen* 37
iodine: *Jod* (n.) 1491
iron: (*n.*, metal): *Eisen* (n.) 1383; (*v.*) *bügeln* 657
island: *Insel* (f.) 1069
it: *es* 62
Italian (*n.*): *Italienisch* 116

jack: *Wagenheber* (m.) 390
jacket: *Jacke* (f.) 1323; dinner —: *Smoking* (m.) 1324
jam: *Marmelade* (f.) 859
janitor: *Hausmeister* (m.) 2128; *Pförtner* (m.) 2160
January: *Januar* (m.) 1986
jaw: *Kiefer* (m.) 1892
jewelry: *Schmuck* (m.) 1556; — store: *Juweliergeschäft* (n.) 1684
job (profession): *Beruf* (m.) 94
joint (body): *Gelenk* (n.) 1893

meter: *Meter* (n.) 1238

middle, in the: *in der Mitte* 211

midnight, at: *mitternachts* 1940

mild: *mild* 836, 1442, 1492

milk: *Milch* (f.) 847

million, one: *Million* (f.) 2040

millionth: *millionste* 2055

mineral water: *Mineralwasser* (n.) 720

minimum charge: *Mindestpreis* (m.) 1166

minister: *Pfarrer* (m.) 1115

minute: *Minute* (f.) 344

mirror: *Spiegel* (m.) 1495; rear-view —: *Innenrückspiegel* (m.) 468; side-view —: *Außenspiegel* (m.) 469

Miss: *Fräulein* 39

miss (a train): *verpassen* 141

missing, be: *fehlen* 173

mistake (*n.*): *Fehler* (m.) 827

modern: *modern* 1084

moment: *Moment* (m.) 30

Monday: *Montag* (m.) 1631

money: *Geld* (n.) 1224; — exchange: *Wechselstube* (f.) 1690; — order: *Postanweisung* (f.) 520

month: *Monat* (m.) 601

monument: *Denkmal* (n.) 219

moped: *Moped* (n.) 366

more: *mehr* 609

morning: *Morgen* (m.) 2; in the —: *morgens* 1935

mosquito net: *Moskitonetz* (n.) 703

mother: *Mutter* (f.) 2067

mother-in-law: *Schwiegermutter* (f.) 2082

motor: *Motor* (m.) 410; — scooter: *Motorroller* (m.) 364

motorcycle: *Motorrad* (n.) 363

mountain: *Berg* (m.) 1221

mountains: *Gebirge* (n.) 1070

mouth: *Mund* (m.) 1901

mouthwash: *Mundwasser* (n.) 1496

movies: *Kino* (n.) 1150

Mr.: *Herr* 37

Mrs.: *Frau* 38

mud: *Schlamm* (m.) 392

part (*n.*, hair): *Scheitel*
(m.) 1623
PARTS OF THE BODY,
p. 146
passport: *Paß* (m.) 154
pastry: *Gebäck* (n.) 856;
— shop: *Konditorei* (f.)
749
paved: *gepflastert* 371
pay (*v.*): *bezahlen* 825,
1300; *zahlen* 1289
peach: *Pfirsich* (m.) 1034
pear: *Birne* (f.) 1023
peas: *Erbsen* (pl.) 961
pea soup: *Erbsensuppe*
(f.) 871
pedal: *Pedal* (n.) 473
pedestrian: *Fußgänger*
(m.) 2119
pediatrician: *Kinderarzt*
(m.) 1716
pen: ballpoint —:
Kugelschreiber (m.)
1429; felt-tip —:
Filzschreiber (m.) 1430;
fountain —: *Füllfeder*
(f.) 1431
pencil: *Bleistift* (m.) 1432
penicillin: *Penicillin* (n.)
1745
penknife: *Taschenmesser*
(n.) 1559

pepper: *Pfeffer* (m.) 838;
green —: *grüne
Paprikaschote* (f.) 968
peppery: *pfeffrig* 790
per: *pro* 270
performance: *Aufführung*
(f.) 2136; *Vorstellung*
(f.) 1141
perfume: *Parfüm* (n.)
1560
perhaps: *vielleicht* 13
permanent wave:
Dauerwelle (f.) 1646
peroxide: *Superoxyd* (n.)
1502
personal: *persönlich* 164
person-to-person call:
Gespräch (n.) *mit
Voranmeldung* 542
pesticide: *Ungezieferver-
tilgungsmittel* (n.) 656
pet shop: *Tierhandlung*
(f.) 1696
pewter: *Zinn* (n.) 1386
PHARMACY, p. 114
pharmacy: *Apotheke* (f.)
1439
photo, take a: *aufnehmen*
1542
photographer:
Photograph (m.) 1697
pick up (retrieve):
abholen 360

181; (hotel) *Hausdiener* (m.) 634

portion: *Portion* (f.) 814

possessions: *Habe* (f.) 643

possible: *möglich* 559

post (*v*.): *ankleben* 2090; *anschlagen* 2092

postage: *Porto* (n.) 512

postcard: *Postkarte* (f.) 512

post office: *Post* (f.) 505

potato: *Kartoffel* (f.) 975; (Austria) *Erdapfel* (m.) 962; baked —: *Kartoffel im Ofen gebraten* 976; boiled —: *Pellkartoffel* 992; *Salzkartoffel* 1005; fried —: *Bratkartoffel* 960; *Pommes frites* (pl.) 995; *Rostkartoffel* 1002; hash-brown —: *Geröstel* (n.) 966; mashed —: *Kartoffelpüree* (n.) 979; (northern Germany and G.D.R.) *Kartoffelbrei* (m.) 974; (Switzerland) *Härdöpfelstock* (m.) 970; — pancakes: *Kartoffelpuffer* (pl.) 978; (Bavaria) *Reiberdatschi* (m.) 999;

(northern and central Germany) *Kartoffelpfannkuchen* (pl.) 977; (Rhineland) *Reibekuchen* (pl.) 998; (Switzerland) *Tätschli* (n.) 1012; — salad: *Kartoffelsalat* (m.) 881; stuffed —: *gefüllte Kartoffel* 964

pottery: *Töpferware* (f.) 1562

POULTRY, p. 78

pound: *Pfund* (n.) 1239

powder: *Puder* (m.) 1503; — puff: *Puderquaste* (f.) 1507

prayer: *Gebet* (n.) 1116; — book: *Gebetbuch* (n.) 1117

precious stone: *Edelstein* (m.) 1563

prefer: (= like) *gern haben* 755; (= would rather have) *lieber mögen* 569

prepare: *zubereiten* 793

prescription: *Rezept* (n.) 1441

press (*v*., = iron): *bügeln* 1588

pressure: *Druck* (m.) 1740

soap: *Seife* (f.) 669
soccer: *Fußball* (m.)
1179; — game:
Fußballspiel (n.) 1193
SOCIAL PHRASES,
p. 3
sock: *Socke* (f.) 1348
soda (water):
Selterswasser (n.) 721
soft: *weich* 857, 1252
soft-boiled: *weichgekocht*
865
sold (= obtainable):
erhältlich 2131
sole: (fish) *Scholle* (f.)
951; *Seezunge* (f.) 953;
(shoe) *Sohle* (f.) 1599
some: *einige* 664; *ein paar*
1569
someone: *jemand* 360
something: *etwas* 604
son: *Sohn* (m.) 2072
soon: *bald* 9
sore (adj.): *wund* 1828
sorry, I'm: *es tut mir leid*
22
SOUPS AND SALADS,
p. 75
soup spoon: *Suppenlöffel*
(m.) 780
south: *Süden* (m.) 193
souvenir: *Andenken* (n.)
1566

spaghetti: *Spaghetti* (pl.)
1008
spark plug: *Zündkerze*
(f.) 486
speak: *sprechen* 113, 114
special delivery, by:
durch Eilboten 509
specialist (medicine):
Facharzt (m.) 1775
specialty: *Spezialität* (f.)
765
speedometer: *Tachometer*
(n.; sometimes m.) 487
spell (v.): *buchstabieren*
129
spicy: *scharf* 791
spinach: *Spinat* (m.) 1011
spine: *Wirbelsäule* (f.)
1913
spit (v.): *spucken* 2177
spleen: *Milz* (f.) 1914
sponge: *Schwamm* (m.)
1522
sporting: — event:
Sportveranstaltung (f.)
1160; — goods store:
Sportgeschäft (n.) 1704
SPORTS AND GAMES,
p. 95
sprain (n.): *Verstauchung*
(f.) 1817
spring: (metal) *Feder* (f.)

1610; (season) *Frühling* (m.) 1998

square (public): *Platz* (m.) 214

stage: *Bühne* (f.) 1135

stain: *Fleck* (m.) 1587

stairs: *Treppe* (f.) 223, 2182

stale: *nicht frisch* 805

stamp (*n.*): *Briefmarke* (f.) 518

standing room: *Stehplatz* (m.) 1161

starch: (*n.*, laundry) *Stärkemehl* (n.) 1586; (*v.*) *stärken* 1589

start (auto): *anspringen* 413

starter: *Anlasser* (m.) 488

stay: *bleiben* 100

steak: *Beefsteak* (n.) 894

steamed: *gedämpft* 804

steel: *Stahl* (m.) 1385; stainless —: *rostfreier Stahl* (m.) 1385

steering wheel: *Lenkrad* (n.) 489

step, watch your: *Vorsicht Stufe* 2186

still (*adv.*): *noch* 517

sting, bee: *Bienenstich* (m.) 1818

stockbroker: *Börsenmakler* (m.) 1705

stocking: *Strumpf* (m.) 1351

stomach: *Magen* (m.) 1762

stone: *Stein* (m.) 1408

stop: (*n.*) *Haltestelle* (f.) 322; (*v.*) *halten* 292, 342; — over (*v.*): *die Reise unterbrechen* 266; — sign: *Stop(p)schild* (n.) 385

store (*n.*): *Laden* (m.) 220

STORES AND SERVICES, p. 130

strap: *Riemen* (m.) 1602

strawberry: *Erdbeere* (f.) 1025

stream: *Bach* (m.) 1223

street: *Straße* (f.) 196

streetcar: *Straßenbahn* (f.) 317

string: *Schnur* (f.) 1435

stroller: *Sportwagen* (m.) 1722

strong: *solid* 1253

stub (ticket): *Kontrollabschnitt* (m.) 1136

stuck: *festgefahren* 392

student: *Student* (m.) 91

tomorrow: *morgen* 1073;
day after —:
übermorgen 1952; —
morning: *morgen früh*
622

tongue: *Zunge* (f.) 1921

tonic (water): *Tonic* (n.)
726

tonight: *heute abend* 570

tonsil: *Mandel* (f.) 1922

tonsillitis: *Mandel-
entzündung* (f.) 1821

too (*adv.*): *zu* 806

tool: *Werkzeug* (n.) 494

tooth: *Zahn* (m.) 1827

toothache: *Zahn-
schmerzen* (pl.) 1830

toothbrush: *Zahnbürste*
(f.) 1529

toothpaste: *Zahnpasta* (f.)
1530

toothpowder: *Zahnpulver*
(n.) 1531

top, at the: *oben* 224

torn: *zerrissen* 1596

tough: *zäh* 806

tour (*n.*): *Rundfahrt* (f.)
1072; guided —:
Führung (f.) 1066

tourist trap: *Touristenfalle*
(f.) 1094

tourniquet: *Aderpresse*
(f.) 1850

tow: *abschleppen* 389

towel: *Handtuch* (n.) 671

town: *Stadt* (f.) 368;
center of —:
Stadtzentrum (n.) 191

toys: *Spielwaren* (f.) 1567

toy shop: *Spielwaren-
geschäft* (n.) 1708

traffic: *Verkehr* (m.) 374;
— circle: *Kreisverkehr*
(m.) 225; — light:
Verkehrsampel (f.) 209

TRAIN, p. 27

train: *Zug* (m.) 141, 2193;
express —: *Fern-
schnellzug* (m.) 288;
local —: *Personen-
zug* (m.) 289; —
station: *Bahnhof* (m.)
213

tranquilizer: *Beruhi-
gungstablette* (f.) 1446

transfer: (*n.*)
Umsteigekarte (f.) 327;
(*v.*) *umsteigen* 325

transit, be in: *auf der
Durchreise sein* 158

transmission: automatic
—: *automatisches
Getriebe* (n.) 495;
standard —: *Stan-
dardgetriebe* (n.) 496

APPENDIX:
COMMON ROAD SIGNS

Gefährliche Kurve.
Dangerous bend.

Kurve rechts.
Right bend.

Kreuzung.
Intersection.

Bahnübergang mit Schranken oder Halbschranken.
Grade-crossing.

Unbeschränkter Bahnübergang.
Grade-crossing without gates.

Lichtzeichenanlage.
Traffic signals ahead.

Baustelle.
Construction.

Fußgängerüberweg.
Pedestrian crossing.

Kinder.
Children.

Wildwechsel.
Animal crossing.

Verengte Fahrbahn.
Road narrows.

Unebene Fahrbahn.
Uneven (OR: Rough) road.

Gefälle.
Steep (OR: Dangerous) hill.

Schleudergefahr bei Nässe oder Schmutz.
Slippery road.

Vorfahrt gewähren.
Yield right-of-way.

Einmündung.
Merging traffic.

Gegenverkehr.
Two-way traffic ahead.

Gefahrzeichen.
Danger.

Steinschlag.
Danger from falling rocks.

Halt! Vorfahrt gewähren.
Stop.

Verbot für Fahrzeuge aller Art.
Closed to all vehicles.

Verbot der Einfahrt.
No entry.

Durchgang für Fußgänger verboten.
Closed to pedestrians.

Links einbiegen verboten.
No left turns.

Wenden verboten.
No U turns.

Überholverbot für Kraftfahrzeuge aller Art.
No passing.

Zulässige Höchstgeschwindigkeit.
Speed limit (OR: Maximum speed).

Hupen verboten.
Use of horn prohibited.

Parken verboten.
No parking.

Haltverbot.
Stopping prohibited.

Einbahnverkehr.
One-way traffic.

Kurven.
Curves.

Kreisverkehr.
Traffic circle.

Sackgasse.
Dead-end.

LISTEN & LEARN CASSETTES

Complete, practical at-home language learning courses for people with limited study time—specially designed for travelers.

Special features:

• Dual-language—Each phrase first in English, then the foreign-language equivalent, followed by a pause for repetition (allows for easy use of cassette even without manual).

• Native speakers—Spoken by natives of the country who are language teachers at leading colleges and universities.

• Convenient manual—Contains every word on the cassettes—all fully indexed for fast phrase or word location.

Each boxed set contains one 90-minute cassette and complete manual.

Listen & Learn French .... Cassette and Manual
99914-9 $8.95

Listen & Learn German .... Cassette and Manual
99915-7 $8.95

Listen & Learn Italian............................... Cassette and Manual
99916-5 $8.95

Listen & Learn Japanese........................ Cassette and Manual
99917-3 $8.95

Listen & Learn Modern Greek .... Cassette and Manual
99921-1 $8.95

Listen & Learn Modern Hebrew .... Cassette and Manual
99923-8 $8.95

Listen & Learn Portuguese...................... Cassette and Manual
99919-X $8.95

Listen & Learn Russian............................ Cassette and Manual
99920-3 $8.95

Listen & Learn Spanish............................ Cassette and Manual
99918-1 $8.95

Listen & Learn Swedish .... Cassette and Manual
99922-X $8.95

Precise, to-the-point guides for adults with limited learning time

ESSENTIAL GRAMMAR SERIES

Designed for independent study or as supplements to conventional courses, the *Essential Grammar* series provides clear explanations of all aspects of grammar—no trivia, no archaic material. Do not confuse these volumes with abridged grammars. These volumes are complete. All volumes 5⅜ × 8¼.

ESSENTIAL FRENCH GRAMMAR, Seymour Resnick. 159pp. °20419-7 Pa. $3.95

ESSENTIAL GERMAN GRAMMAR, Guy Stern and E. F. Bleiler. 124pp. °20422-7 Pa. $3.50

ESSENTIAL ITALIAN GRAMMAR, Olga Ragusa. 111pp. °20779-X Pa. $3.50

ESSENTIAL JAPANESE GRAMMAR, E. F. Bleiler. 156pp. 21027-8 Pa. $3.50

ESSENTIAL PORTUGUESE GRAMMAR, Alexander da R. Prista. 114pp. 21650-0 Pa. $3.95

ESSENTIAL SPANISH GRAMMAR, Seymour Resnick. 115pp. °20780-3 Pa. $3.50

ESSENTIAL MODERN GREEK GRAMMAR, Douglas Q. Adams. 128pp. 25133-0 Pa. $4.50

ESSENTIAL DUTCH GRAMMAR, Henry R. Stern. 110pp. 24675-2 Pa. $4.50

ESSENTIAL ENGLISH GRAMMAR, Philip Gucker. 177pp. 21649-7 Pa. $3.95

°Not available in British Commonwealth Countries except Canada.